T0419675

BETTY FORD: A SYMBOL OF STRENGTH

OTHER BOOKS IN THE PRESIDENTIAL WIVES SERIES

Dolley Madison
Paul M. Zall
2001. ISBN 1-56072-930-9. (Hardcover)
2001. ISBN 1-56072-937-6. (Softcover)

A "Bully" First Lady: Edith Kermit Roosevelt
Tom Lansford
2001. ISBN 1-59033-086-2. (Hardcover)
2003. ISBN 1-56072-648-8. (Softcover)

Sarah Childress Polk, First Lady of Tennessee and Washington
Barbara Bennett Peterson
2002. ISBN 1-59033-145-1. (Hardcover)
2002. ISBN 1-56072-551-1. (Softcover)

Frances Clara Folsom Cleveland
Stephen F. Robar
2002. ISBN 1-59033-245-8. (Hardcover)

Lucretia
John Shaw
2002. ISBN 1-59033-349-7. (Hardcover)

Betty Ford: A Symbol of Strength
Jeffrey S. Ashley
2003. ISBN 1-59033-407-8(Hardcover)

BETTY FORD: A SYMBOL OF STRENGTH

JEFFREY S. ASHLEY

Nova History Publications, Inc.
New York

Senior Editors: Susan Boriotti and Donna Dennis
Coordinating Editor: Tatiana Shohov
Office Manager: Annette Hellinger
Graphics: Wanda Serrano
Editorial Production: Vladimir Klestov, Matthew Kozlowski and Maya Columbus
Circulation: Ave Maria Gonzalez, Vera Popovic, Luis Aviles, Raymond Davis,
Melissa Diaz and Jeannie Pappas
Communications and Acquisitions: Serge P. Shohov
Marketing: Cathy DeGregory

Library of Congress Cataloging-in-Publication Data
Available Upon Request

ISBN 1-59033-407-8.

Copyright © 2003 by Nova History Publications, a division of
Nova Science Publishers, Inc.
400 Oser Ave, Suite 1600
Hauppauge, New York 11788-3619
Tele.: 631-231-7269   Fax: 631-231-8175
e-mail: Novascience@earthlink.net
Web Site: http://www.novapublishers.com

All rights reserved. No part of this book may be reproduced, stored in a retrieval system or transmitted in any form or by any means: electronic, electrostatic, magnetic, tape, mechanical photocopying, recording or otherwise without permission from the publishers.

The authors and publisher have taken care in preparation of this book, but make no expressed or implied warranty of any kind and assume no responsibility for any errors or omissions. No liability is assumed for incidental or consequential damages in connection with or arising out of information contained in this book.

This publication is designed to provide accurate and authoritative information with regard to the subject matter covered herein. It is sold with the clear understanding that the publisher is not engaged in rendering legal or any other professional services. If legal or any other expert assistance is required, the services of a competent person should be sought. FROM A DECLARATION OF PARTICIPANTS JOINTLY ADOPTED BY A COMMITTEE OF THE AMERICAN BAR ASSOCIATION AND A COMMITTEE OF PUBLISHERS.

Printed in the United States of America

CONTENTS

Foreword		**vii**
	Robert P. Watson	
Preface		**xi**
Acknowledgments		**xiii**
Part 1:	**Pre-White House**	**1**
Chapter 1	**Early Years**	**3**
	Important Highlights	*9*
Chapter 2	**Teens and Early Adulthood**	**11**
	Teens	*11*
	Early Adulthood	*19*
	Important Highlights	*23*
Chapter 3	**Gerald R. Ford, Jr.**	**25**
	Important Highlights	*32*
Chapter 4	**New Job, New Family**	**35**
	Congress	*35*
	The Ford Family	*39*
	Important Highlights	*46*
Chapter 5	**Betty's Identity**	**49**
Chapter 6	**1964-1973**	**57**
Part 2:	**The Executive Branch**	**65**
Chapter 7	**One Step-Away**	**67**

Chapter 8	**A New Era**	**75**
Chapter 9	**The Symbolic Role**	**83**
Chapter 10	**Betty's Causes**	**93**
	The Press Conference and Support for Equal Rights	*93*
	Cancer and Being a Role Model	*96*
Chapter 11	**Election Hopes**	**101**
Part 3:	**Post-White House**	**111**
Chapter 12	**A New Life**	**113**
Chapter 13	**The Ford Legacy**	**121**
	Jerry's Legacy	*121*
	Betty's Legacy	*124*
Bibliography		**129**
Notes		**133**
Index		**137**

FOREWORD

The old saying that "behind every successful man is a woman" is perhaps nowhere more evident than in the White House. Even a cursory examination of the wives of presidents reveals a group of remarkable individuals who made many contributions to the lives and careers of their husbands, the presidency, and even the nation. Over the course of U.S. history first ladies have presided over state dinners, overseen extensive historical renovations of the Executive Mansion, held press conferences, campaigned for their husbands, testified before Congress, championed important social causes, and addressed the United Nations.

As a candidate for the presidency speaking of the role his wife would assume in his administration Bill Clinton stated that when the public elects a president, they are getting "two for the price of one!" To an extent such a statement has always been true. First ladies have been a viable part of the presidency since the nation's founding. Of the men who served as president during the country's history, nearly all of them served with a first lady at their side. Only a handful of presidents have held the office without their spouses. For instance, both Andrew Jackson and Chester A. Arthur had lost their wives prior to their presidencies; Rachel Jackson dying in the interim between her husband's election and his inauguration and Ellen Arthur just prior to her husband's Vice Presidency. The wives of both Thomas Jefferson and Martin Van Buren passed away years before their presidencies. But they were exceptions. Only two bachelor presidents have been elected, Grover Cleveland and James Buchanan, however the former married while in office. Three presidential wives died while serving in the White House: Letitia Tyler, Caroline Harrison, and Ellen Wilson. However, both President John Tyler and President Woodrow Wilson later remarried while in office.

Presidential wives have served without pay and, until very recently, often without proper recognition. So too have they wielded political power and social influence despite the fact that they are neither elected nor appointed. In part because they are not elected or accountable to the citizenry and in part because of strict social conventions that precluded women from participating in politics for much of the nation's history, presidential wives have been forced to exercise their power and influence in a behind-the-scenes manner. Yet, in this capacity many wives have functioned as their husband's trusted confidante and private political advisor.

Presidential wives have faced great challenges, not the least of which include the loss of privacy and specter of assassination looming for themselves and their families. The presidency is arguably the most demanding job in the country and the challenges of the office are experienced by the president's family. Amazingly, several first ladies served while trying to raise a family. Presidential wives have faced severe scrutiny, an invasive press corps and curious public, and criticism from journalists and the president's political enemies. This is perhaps one of the experiences that all first ladies have shared. Not even popular wives like Martha Washington, Abigail Adams, or Jacqueline Kennedy were spared from harsh personal attacks.

The first ladyship has been the "unknown institution" of the White House. For most of its history it has been ignored by scholars and overlooked by those studying national and presidential politics. However, this is slowly changing. The public, press, and scholars are beginning to take note of the centrality of the first lady to the presidency. A new view of the president's spouse as a "partner" in the presidency is replacing more traditional views of presidential wives. Even though the Founding Fathers of the country gave no thought to the president's wife and the Constitution is silent concerning her duties, today the "office" has become a powerful, recognized institution within the presidency, complete with staff and budgetary resources that rival the so-called "key" presidential advisors.

It is also an intriguing office whose occupants are no less fascinating themselves. Indeed, the presidential wives are a diverse lot that includes new brides barely out of their teens to grandmothers who had spent a lifetime married to men that would become president. There have been women of refinement and wealth and there have been wives who would seem ill-prepared for the challenges of the White House. And of course, there have been successes and there have been failures.

The first ladyship is one of the nation's most challenging and dynamic public offices. So too is it an office still in development. In the words of First Lady Barbara Bush, concluding her remarks when delivering the commencement speech at Wellesley College, "And who knows? Somewhere out in this audience may even be someone who will one day follow in my footsteps, and preside over the White House as the President's spouse. I wish *him* well!"

In the volumes of this Series the reader will find the stories of women who fashioned the course of American history. It is the goal of the publishers and myself that this book and each volume in the Presidential Wives Series shed light on this important office and reveal the lives of the women behind the American presidency.

I hope you enjoy this book and the entire Series!

Robert P. Watson, Series Editor

PREFACE

Betty Ford is remembered as one of the most outspoken and influential first ladies of all time. Although she entered the White House during turbulent times, Mrs. Ford captivated a nation and provided them with someone they could trust. Serving immediately following the Watergate scandal meant that she would be subjected to greater scrutiny than most of her predecessors. Fortunately for the country, Mrs. Ford did not shy away from the challenge. Her positive attitude, candor, and honesty were refreshing remedies for an ailing nation and set the standard for the modern first lady.

What most people do not realize is that Mrs. Ford has been through a complete make-over at key points in her life. She has, in a sense, been through three distinct life periods — her life leading up to the time she met Gerald Ford and went to Congress as part of a political partnership is the first part of her journey. The second phase of her life was one in which she almost lost her sense of individuality and suffered the consequences. This period evolved between the time she and Jerry left for Washington, D.C. and the time that she developed breast cancer while serving as the First Lady of the United States. It was this key event which triggered the third phase of Betty Ford's life. The support she received made Betty Ford aware of the fact that she had a powerful voice and could become the outspoken champion for many issues. While her recovery from addiction could very well be considered yet a fourth phase, her devotion to the cause of alcohol and drug addiction really follows along with her enthusiastic support for women's rights, breast cancer awareness, and other social concerns — issues she addressed while first lady and has never abandoned.

Throughout her life, each segment has been critical in setting Betty Ford up to become one of our greatest first ladies ever. A unique feature of this book is that, at least for the early stages of her development, the highlights of that period are set aside at the end of each chapter. After reading about a particular period of her life, the reader is focused on the impact that this had on Betty Ford as a person and on her ability to later serve as first lady in the manner that she did. While this is done for only a select few chapters, it is helpful in setting the tone for the remainder of the text.

Another feature of this book is that it is written for a general audience and is presented in a non-academic format. As such, citations have been kept to a minimum by only citing direct quotes. However, a number of sources were used in the writing of this book and readers would do themselves a favor by taking the time to examine the bibliography in order to give proper credit to the many people who have had wonderful things to say about Betty Ford.

It is my sincere hope that the audience will enjoy reading this short biography as much as I have enjoyed writing it! Betty Ford is quite simply an extraordinary woman and a symbol of strength for us all.

ACKNOWLEDGMENTS

I would like to thank Mrs. Ford for graciously allowing me to interview her and for granting me the right to borrow extensively from her two autobiographies. This was especially helpful for her early years. Since most of the literature and biographical information on Mrs. Ford didn't start to emerge until later on in her life, developing a framework for seeing who she has become as a person would have been impossible without her insight. Thank you!

I would also like to thank Robert Watson, the editor of the Presidential Wives Series. The opportunity to do research on Betty Ford would never have emerged if Dr. Watson had not urged me to look into it. I will always be thankful to Bob for pressing me into studying such a magnificent woman as Betty Ford. Bob, you are a great colleague and an even better friend.

I cannot ignore the faculty in the department of political science at Eastern Illinois University. Rich Wandling, Melinda Mueller, Barb Poole, Ryan Hendrickson, Andy McNitt, Dave Carwell, Ed Brazil, Lillian Barria, and Steve Roper are one of the greatest groups of people I have ever met. Thank you for welcoming me to the department and for making Eastern a home!

Finally, I would like to extend my deepest thanks and gratitude to my wife, Leslie, for her love and support and to our daughter, Rachel, for her wonderful smiles. Leslie, looking at the back of my head has not been easy for you, but I appreciate your support. Rachel, you are only two months old, but your support has been critical too. The two of you are definitely what keeps me going.

PART 1: PRE-WHITE HOUSE

Chapter 1

EARLY YEARS

Born on April 8, 1918 in Chicago, Illinois, Betty was the youngest of William and Hortense Bloomer's three children. Her brothers Bill and Bob were actually quite a bit older than Betty — Bill by seven years, and Bob by five. It seems that Betty was somewhat of a surprise and was the result of an unplanned party. In fact, her mother often remarked that Betty had popped out of a bottle of champagne. While the idea seemed charming and held a certain appeal for Betty, there may have been some truth to the statement since Hortense was in her mid-thirties when Betty was born. While that is not unusual by today's standards, it was a bit older than the average childbearing age in 1918. Nevertheless, Elizabeth Ann was a welcome addition to the Bloomer family.

Early in Betty's life the family moved from Chicago to Denver but eventually landed in Grand Rapids, Michigan when she was two years old. Grand Rapids was a bustling Midwestern community and it was at 717 Fountain Street that Betty would spend her formative years with her mother, father, and two older brothers.

Little has been said or written about Betty Ford's father, William. A salesman for the Royal Rubber company, William was away from home quite often. He seems to have played much less of a role in Betty's life than her mother, Hortense. This is not to say that Betty did not love her dad — quite the contrary, Betty adored William. When he was home, she would stay close to him and soak in whatever bits and pieces of attention she could get. She also paid very close attention to her father's actions. In her autobiography, *The Times of My Life*, she recalls his excitement over dialing in other cities on an old crystal radio set and calling the children around to listen. This was one of his favorite pastimes and it was something that he and the kids shared together.

Betty did, however, regret not getting to spend more time with her father. William probably felt similar pangs of remorse. He really was gone for much of the children's lives. He apparently felt bad about missing out on the children's upbringing and tried to ease his guilt through material means. When he was home, he showered the children with gifts. One gift that stands out was a little brown teddy bear. Perhaps the bear reminded Betty of her father, or maybe she simply adored the bear. In any case, Betty became attached to that bear and dragged it along with her wherever she went. Many pictures of her youth include the little brown bear that, to her, was very much alive.

Gifts aside, Betty was not about to let her father buy his way out of her feelings of sadness. Bears are nice, but little girls want their fathers. According to Betty, he was "trying to make up for his absences."[1] It is clear that Betty never truly understood her father's frequent departures and she swore, at an early age, that she would grow up and marry a man who stayed at home.

William did manage to take long periods of time off of work during the summer and the family would leave for Whitefish Lake. The family owned a small cottage at the lake and could be found there from the time school let out in the spring until classes began again in the fall. Betty loved the times spent at the lake and recalls many fun times. Many of the experiences from her summers at the lake would influence Betty later in life. For instance, Betty developed her lifelong distaste for fish while spending time at Whitefish Lake. William was an avid fisherman who was also very successful when it came to angling. The result was that the Bloomer family had a lot of fish to consume. According to Betty, "we were served fish, fish, and more fish until I hoped I would never see fish again."[2] Later in life, Betty would be in control of her own family menus and she did not include fish. She would not cook it, and would only order it at a restaurant under very rare occasions. This is not to say that Betty did not eat and did not enjoy food — just not fish.

There was a hotel near the Bloomer cottage that was surrounded by picnic grounds which Betty would often frequent. At the picnic grounds, there were people eating foods that Betty did like! Betty became quite adept at making the picnic ground rounds and picking up little snacks and morsels of food from each of the campers. Of course, as a little girl, many of her favorites included cookies and ice cream — childhood health food. The result was that Betty became a little bit chunky as a small child. According to Betty, "my mother was an attractive woman, my father was a good looking man, and I was a fat little kid."[3] At one point, Hortense resorted to hanging a sign around Betty's neck which urged the campers: "Please do not feed this child."[4]

Of course there were other things to do at the lake besides eat. As the family spent several summers at the cottage, there was the opportunity for Betty and her brothers to make a number of friends and to engage in any number of summertime outdoor activities. The children would spend countless hours swimming in the lake becoming, in Betty's word, "demon swimmers." They also engaged in the universal outdoor tradition of the snipe hunt. Betty was initiated at a young age and, along with her brothers and other children around Whitefish Lake, dutifully carried on the snipe tradition by terrorizing other youngsters each year. For those unfamiliar with a snipe hunt, it is really nothing more than a way for older kids to have fun at the expense of younger children who don't know any better than to believe in snipes. When all is said and done, however, the snipe hunt allows for children to become better friends and to bond with one another.

The bonds formed at Whitefish Lake would last a lifetime. The joy of summertime coupled with a large group of good people simply endured the test of time. Many of these friendships have been passed on from generation to generation and the community of Whitefish Lake is a close one indeed. In her first memoir, *The Times of My Life*, Betty recalls the people from her annual summer vacation by stating:

> It was a tight-knit community; most of the people we knew there have held on to their families cottages, and today they go up with their grandchildren. The members of my generation feel a closeness that comes from our parents' having been friends, and of our having shared long summers when our world was as green as our hopes. Mostly we haven't seen each other for years, but if by chance two of us meet we start right in to chatter as though we'd been together yesterday.[5]

Of course, the relationships built between Betty and other children were not the only bonds being forged at Whitefish Lake. Betty formed a very strong relationship with her mother. While the bond was strengthened year-round, Betty remembers her mother's strength and warmth from the lake with special fondness. Weather tends to be enhanced when one is outdoors, and storms at the lake were no exception. Wind, lightning, thunder, and rain all seem to become magnified and appear to be much more threatening outside the comforts of one's home. It was during some of these storms that Hortense really showed her strength and Betty learned to love and respect her mother at a different level. According to Betty, as told to Chris Chase in *Times of My Life*,

> I can still feel my mother's arms around me, holding me, as she stood out on the porch and we watched a storm rolling in across the lake, waves swelling,

thunder crashing, lightning slicing the sky, and my mother telling me how beautiful it was. I found out later she was scared to death, but she taught me not to be afraid; I was safe in those arms.[6]

Betty and Hortense shared something special!

Back home in Grand Rapids, the mother-daughter bond between Hortense and Betty would continue to develop and grow over the years. While William was away, which was most of the time, Hortense was given the primary responsibility of raising the children. Hortense was a very commanding figure who had a certain air about her that impacted those around her. According to one of Betty's childhood friends, Lillian Fisher, "all she had to do was just stand there and you stood a little straighter too and sort of shaped up."

Hortense tended to be very formal and strict with her daughter — from the way she dressed, to table manners, to even chewing gum (which could not be done in the presence of others). She even demanded that Betty wear white gloves and a hat whenever they went downtown to shop. That the other little girls were not required to dress in a similar fashion mattered little to Hortense. She simply informed Betty that her mores were not necessarily the mores of Grand Rapids.

Aside from manners and decorum, Hortense was influential in other ways too. Being the only constant parent meant that Hortense had to be the disciplinarian and she was often very hard on Betty. In later years, Betty would demand quite a bit of herself as a result of the unintentional pressures placed on her by her mother. Hortense was a very hard act to follow despite Betty's best efforts. One such area of influence stemmed from Hortense's opinion that anything worth doing was worth doing right! This insistence on perfection was illustrated early on during Betty's school days. After one of her school shows, in which Betty did not perform up to her mother's standards, Hortense stated, "if you don't do it well, don't do it at all."[7] While Betty was undoubtedly hurt by the comment, it made her work harder and strive for greater things in the future.

Hortense also had a softer side and knew how to make Betty feel special. Betty simply loved the ongoing story that she had "popped out of a bottle of champagne." Hortense also knew how to instill a sense of pride in her daughter when Betty was feeling down. A prime example is the time Betty came home from school crying because the other children had teased her about the birthmark on her arm. Hortense turned the situation around and stated that because Betty was the only girl with that particular mark, she was a "very special child." That statement allowed Betty to return to school the next day with her head held high — after all, she was unique. The combination of strict formality coupled with a loving intuition helped Betty and Hortense to develop a special bond. Betty worshiped her mother and wanted to be like her. In later years, Betty would form a similar bond with her own daughter.

Overall, her childhood appears to have been happy and full of fond memories. From jumping through piles of leaves in the fall to swimming in Whitefish Lake in the summer, Betty was a typical child who enjoyed playing with friends and family. In her words, "there were few shadows over my childhood." In particular, Betty enjoyed spending time with her older brothers — much to their chagrin. In fact, there was a time when Betty became something of a tomboy while following her brothers around pestering them to let her play sports with them and the other boys. Betty took to playing sports such as hockey and football in order to try and spend more time with her older siblings. Betty even joined them on the annual Halloween rampage they called "garbage night." Instead of trick or treating, they would terrorize the neighborhood by tipping over garbage cans, whitewashing porches, and soaping windows. While under the care of Bill and Bob, Betty also developed a lifelong tendency to root for the underdog. Whenever they would fight, she would inevitably get involved by pulling off the guy on top — regardless of which brother happened to be winning. She didn't care who won, she just rooted for the individual who happened to be losing at the time.

Growing up with brothers in a small home with only one bathroom led to Betty being something less than modest. She thought nothing of running across the hall with no clothes on — after all, this was just family. As she got a little older, however, such a practice was troubling to Hortense who prided her self on propriety. At one point Hortense finally informed Betty that she had to start putting some clothes on. Betty was still fairly young and the request was confusing to her and was, at best, a ridiculous notion. Hortense would not be dissuaded. She suggested to Betty that her brothers might start bringing some of their friends home and that it simply would not do for them to see Betty running around naked. Hortense bought Betty a robe and that was the end of it. Betty obliged her mother but she remained just one of the guys as far as she was concerned.

While Betty loved her brothers and being a tomboy seemed only natural to her, Hortense, being the formal woman that she was, didn't seem too particularly keen on the idea. In an attempt to teach her daughter to be more graceful and ladylike, Hortense thought that she might take a different approach with her daughter and introduce her to the arts. Something very important happened to Betty when she was only eight years old — something which would guide her through her early twenties and the rest of her life — she discovered dance.

When Betty was eight, she and a group of other children began taking social dance classes and, while all of the kids were doing it, dancing proved to be something special for her. She loved dancing and approached it with gusto. Despite the fact that her initial recital was nothing spectacular — her mother thought Betty wasn't very good and should give it up — Betty persevered. She continued to study dance with Calla Travis, the local dance instructor, throughout her childhood. According to Mrs. Ford, "dance was my happiness."[8]

Little Betty also loved being a socialite and competitor for the boys' attention. Apparently the youngsters had a competition wherein the big thing was to get "engaged." However, for the engagement to be official, the boy had to give them a ring with something resembling a diamond in it. This couldn't be just any ring either — it had to come from Woolworth's. These girls were very particular about the quality of the jewelry they received! When Betty was ten years old, after one of Calla Travis' dance recitals, she got engaged to Bud Wilmarth. He promised to meet her after the recital with the ring and she kept her mother waiting, wondering where Betty was. Ever the competitor, she wasn't about to leave the recital hall without the ring. After all, Bud Wilmarth was the one boy that all of the girls were after. She was only ten and was already a hit with the boys and was establishing herself as quite the dancer.

Betty was eleven when the stock market crashed in 1929 and started the nation towards the Great Depression. The Bloomers took a financial hit along with most of the country and William Bloomer took the losses extremely hard. According to Betty's brother, Bill, "I remember, very vividly, the pain he showed from not being able to do everything."[9] If William showed strain from his inability to take care of his family in the manner he desired, Hortense showed no such pressure. As was her style, she simply carried on as if things were exactly the way they were supposed to be. Just as she played the courageous mother at Whitefish Lake, she played the strong mother figure at home in Grand Rapids during the depression. She began to work outside the home to help make ends meet and encouraged the rest of the family to cut back in any way they could — they would get along just fine. One of the downsides to the depression was that the family was forced to let go of the cottage at Whitefish Lake that had brought them so many fond memories over the years. To a group raised by Hortense Bloomer, however, such a loss was hardly noticed since they were all busy working to help out in any way they could. Betty hardly noticed because she was preoccupied with boys and dancing.

Betty went to her first dance with a boy when she was twelve years old. Given the strictness of her mother, it would seem unlikely that she would permit Betty to do such a thing as a young girl. However, Betty was accompanied by her two older brothers so Hortense felt much more at ease with the situation. What Hortense didn't know was that Bill and Bob were not exactly planning on keeping an eye on her so much as they wanted to lose her. Nothing was likely to happen anyway since she was twelve and her "date" was one of her brother's friends — a young man named Bill Warren. Betty was just thrilled to have the chance to go hear one of the traveling big bands that was touring the country at the time — in this case, the Wayne King band.

What more could a girl want than to get the chance to hear live music and to dance?

Hortense still had the final say-so on the dress Betty would wear. The dress was Betty's first formal, long, dress and was much too plain for her tastes. Betty wanted something more elegant to suit the importance of the occasion while Hortense opted for a more conservative approach (Betty was, after all, only twelve). Hortense won the battle. Nevertheless, Betty was off for her first date and starting to make the transition from childhood into adolescence. The once chubby little girl who opted for sports instead of "girl stuff," and who enjoyed causing mischief on snipe hunts and on "garbage night," was beginning to soften. The tomboy was becoming a young woman and Grand Rapids would never be the same.

IMPORTANT HIGHLIGHTS

While Betty generally enjoyed her childhood, there are a few points that need to be emphasized once again. People tend to develop character traits early on in their lives and Betty Ford is no exception. Several events from her childhood would dictate how she grew later and how she would handle situations as an adult. One such event, or rather series of events, has to do with her father, William. His frequent absences had a profound impact on Betty later on when she was both a young woman and mother. Despite the fact that she vowed to never marry a man that was frequently absent, this is precisely the type of man she married — twice. This left her alone to handle home and family — much as her mother had done. This brings us to another product of her youth that requires additional attention. The image of her mother as a strong woman who could handle every situation would haunt Betty as she tried, in vain, to be like her mother. As a mature woman saddled with many responsibilities later in life, Betty would buckle under the pressure of trying to do everything by herself. She had a subconscious image in her mind of how a wife and mother handled things and she simply could not live up to that standard. Hortense probably couldn't either but that is not the impression that Betty got as a child, and that is the image that shaped her. Finally, her introduction to dancing would create many opportunities for Betty later on in life and would move her in directions that she might not have otherwise gone. These opportunities and unique directions were more of those life situations that determine who a person is to become.

Chapter 2

TEENS AND EARLY ADULTHOOD

TEENS

Fourteen was an age that marked several important milestones for Betty. For one, it was the year that she started wearing store-bought clothes. Up until then, Hortense had made all of Betty's clothing and Betty had looked forward to the purchases with great anticipation. Looking back, Betty realizes that her mother's clothes were better. At the time, however, Betty didn't realize the craftsmanship that went into her mother's work. In her words, "store-bought dresses weren't as nice as what my mother made me, but when you're brought up by a fine seamstress, you don't appreciate the handiwork."[1] While Betty tried to emulate Hortense in other ways, sewing was not one of them. Betty never did learn how to sew very well and never really cared to.

Fourteen also marked Betty's confirmation into the Episcopal Church. One might think that since her father was a Christian Scientist, and her mother an Episcopalian, the decision to be confirmed was a tough one. Not so. Given the closeness of Betty and Hortense, coupled with the fact that Betty had friends who belonged to the church, becoming an Episcopalian was probably a foregone conclusion. Becoming confirmed in the church was just one more way in which Betty was an ordinary child — living during somewhat turbulent times.

When Betty was fourteen, the nation was engulfed in the Great Depression but the Bloomers were not hit as hard as most. Despite the fact that William took the losses hard and the family was forced to sell its summer cottage at Whitefish Lake, the family was not starving. All of the children did their part to contribute to the household and Hortense took to doing some domestic work to help out. They were, however, able to continue to lead a fairly normal middle class existence.

Betty was able to dabble in music lessons trying both the piccolo and the piano but didn't really take to either one. For Betty, the one thing that inspired her was dancing!

From the time she started taking lessons from Calla Travis at the age of eight, Betty was hooked. Fortunately, she was able to continue taking lessons — even when finances were a little tighter than they had been during the 1920s. Betty went far beyond the social dance classes that her mother felt might teach her gracefulness and some semblance of what a young lady should act like. It didn't matter what the particular form of dance was, Betty loved it all. Calla Travis offered ballet, tap, Spanish dancing, modern dance, etc. Betty signed up for everything and approached her art with a tremendous amount of enthusiasm. In fact, Betty had plans to become a professional dancer.

To help out with the expense of her lessons, Betty began to work a couple of jobs. One job was as a teenage model at Herpolsheimer's Department store. Betty would put on various outfits from the store and wander through the tearoom so that people could admire the latest fashions. Her job was simply to make the clothes look good and to point people in the right direction to obtain the merchandise. The only requirements seemed to be that Betty look presentable and be able to remember the correct department and price of the clothes. Betty did not make a whole lot at the job — three dollars for the afternoon (she worked on Saturdays). Since the money wasn't too great, Betty would leave her checks at the store and would pick them up every few weeks or so once they had accumulated and amounted to something. Of course, this was the Depression and every little bit helped — at least Betty felt better about assisting with her own upkeep.

Another job that Betty tackled was one of her own making. Betty became quite the little entrepreneur by teaching dance classes. Since Calla was the master and was established, Betty felt that she needed to charge less — rightly so. Since Calla charged her students one dollar per lesson, Betty charged her dance pupils fifty cents. Betty "rented" out the basement of a family friend (Flo Jones) for one dollar. Mrs. Jones had told Betty it wasn't the money so much as it was a lesson for Betty. She told Betty that "if you're going into business, you have to start right and understand how businesses are run."[2] In this case, Mrs. Jones was talking about overhead — the steep overhead cost of one dollar. Betty paid the same amount to her friend, Wally Hook, to play piano for the lessons. With a rented hall and a piano player, Betty was in business.

The "Betty Bloomer School of Dance" was open for business every Saturday afternoon (after Betty got off from Herpolsheimer's). Calla wasn't upset with the lost business as hers was a thriving operation and Betty merely eased some of the

Teens and Early Adulthood

burden and allowed Calla to focus more attention on some of her more advanced students — one of whom was Betty.

Prior to her teaching, Betty had to complete the series of courses offered by Calla Travis. Once the series was completed, Calla permitted her students to consider themselves bona fide dance instructors. A requirement for finishing the series, however, was that each student had to complete a solo ballet number. Ordinarily this would be a very small feat for one of Calla's advanced students, but Betty was never ordinary. Despite the fact that Betty planned on becoming a professional dancer, she wasn't exactly the greatest ballerina in town. Her forte was in the less precise and rigid forms of dance. In ballet, each movement is prescribed and requires perfect form. Betty's problem was that she could never get her knees straight — a pretty serious problem for a ballerina. To get around her flaw in form, Betty designed a costume for her solo number that covered her knees. Instead of the traditional tutu, Betty had an outfit with scarves hanging down so that nobody could see that her knees were bent or straight. Once the number was over, Betty was a dance instructor.

As she grew older, Betty became more and more enamored with dance — especially the more fluid modern dance and non-traditional forms of the art. If she heard of some local kid who had been out West and had learned an American Indian dance, Betty would hunt him/her down and have them teach it to her. Of course, this ignored the religious component inherent to many Native dances but, to Betty, dance was dance. She viewed all types of dancing as art forms which needed to be experienced. When she encountered modern dance, she was hooked. Once she discovered the freedom of movement and the fluid nature of this type of dance, ballet school was out of the question. Betty still dreamt of becoming a professional dancer, she just didn't plan on being a ballerina — it was too precise and her knees wouldn't cooperate anyway.

When Betty wasn't working or taking dance lessons, she occupied her time as most adolescent girls did in the 1930s, with school and boys. Betty loved school and was most fond of her language classes — particularly French and Latin. She also liked the social aspect of school. Betty attended Central High in Grand Rapids and was a member of Gamma Delta Tau sorority.

Much like the college fraternities and sororities of today, the groups of Betty's day made potential members go through all of the rigors of pledging — which Betty likened to another snipe hunt since older members delighted in making fools out of the younger ones. These groups were very much socially oriented and were geared towards exclusion to a certain degree. If a group didn't like a person, that individual would not be let into the organization and might feel left out. At the time, Betty and the others thought nothing of it — it was simply the ways things were done. Looking back, Betty sees that, perhaps, some pupils might have been excluded but she still reflects fondly on her days with Gamma Delta Tau — otherwise known as "The Good Cheers."

Many of the members remain in contact and will always be friends. When Betty Ford wrote her first autobiography, *The Times of My Life*, one of her former sorority sisters kindly reminded her, "don't forget The Good Cheers." Betty didn't.

About the time that Betty was a Good Cheer, she and a friend went downtown and had their fortunes told by a woman who read tea leaves. Betty was told that, when she grew up, she would dine with kings and queens. To Betty, this meant that her dream of professional dance was to come true. The fortune was only reinforcing what she already knew — she would make it as a dancer. Of course, the fortuneteller was correct, but not in the way that a young Betty Bloomer could have imagined.

The Good Cheers also engaged in some competition amongst themselves, and with other girls. This competition — continuing from earlier years — centered around young men. According to Betty, she was something of a flirt and was mostly interested in those young men who posed a challenge. She would set her sights on some poor fellow and would go after him until she got his fraternity pin. Once she had the pin, the challenge was over. She would break up with the young man (of course he would get his pin back) and move on to the next guy. The only ones that truly interested Betty were the ones she couldn't get. In *The Times of My Life*, Betty recalls that "sometimes there was a boy who wasn't interested, and that annoyed me. I had crushes on boys I couldn't get dates with." There was one such boy named Dick May and Betty actually got into a fight over him with another girl — he couldn't have cared less. And that made him all the more appealing to Betty. Finally, Dick did something to Betty that his father felt was rude and warranted an apology. Of course when Dick came calling to apologize, bearing a box of candy, any chance of a relationship ended. He ceased to be a challenge.

Betty dated a number of young men in high school but none of them were ever very serious. She has stated that none of her friends had steady boyfriends and she, in particular, had no use for any commitment. She still had her sights on a career in dance, and any type of serious relationship might put her move to New York in jeopardy. This did not stop her from having fun and developing fond memories that would last a lifetime. She looks back on the time she spent with young men such as Bud Wilmarth, Walt Jones, Jack Stiles, Monty Welch, and Louis De Lamarter, and realizes that these were indeed special times. From the time that Monty Welch was so determined to get Betty a piece of frozen cake that he cut through the plate (which was somewhat embarrassing for her) to the times that she went with Louis and his family to see the Michigan Wolverines play football in Ann Arbor, Betty simply led a good existence. According to Mrs. Ford, "I've said I had a sunny childhood. I also had a wonderful girlhood."[3]

These fun times and an active social life would actually become great assets when Betty was the first lady. Being able to feel comfortable around people, and to have them feel at ease, is a necessary skill in the White House — one that Betty learned from her times in Grand Rapids as one of the Good Cheers.

Despite the happiness that surrounded her youth and adolescence, a dark cloud would emerge when Betty was sixteen. Betty and a friend were out driving around in the friend's convertible having a good time when they rolled up on Betty's house. While they were yelling and giggling and generally carrying on, one of Betty's cousins came out and told them to be quiet. Her cousin, Shine, came to tell Betty that something had happened to her father and that he had been taken to the hospital. What wasn't said, was that William was dead. In fact, William had died before the ambulance even arrived at the Bloomer's house.

There is some speculation that William Bloomer's death was a suicide. There is evidence that he was an alcoholic and there is no question that he had been hit hard by the financial losses created by the stock market crash. While rumors of the suicide circulated, family members discount such a notion and attribute William's carbon monoxide poisoning to accidental exposure and unfortunate circumstances. In Betty's autobiography, *The Times of My Life*, she discusses how it was a hot humid day, and that the doors to the garage were open. Her brother Bill asserts that the talk of suicide was nonsense and that proof of the accidental death can be found through the eyes of the insurance company. William had a good deal of life insurance and since suicide invalidates any claims, insurance companies tend to investigate any suspicious circumstances. Since the insurance company paid off on William's policy, according to Bill, it would seem that suicide was out of the question.

It was at the funeral that Betty learned of her father's alcoholism — she was shocked. He never drank at home but apparently did so while traveling. Since he traveled a lot, there was ample opportunity to imbibe. While Betty and the children didn't know about William's drinking, Hortense certainly did. She filled the classic enabler role and protected both William (from the children's ire), and the children (from the truth). After all, Hortense was always extremely protective of those around her.

The family carried on and managed the best they could. They had all been working anyway, and the insurance money made it so that Hortense was a bit more financially secure. Hortense dabbled in real estate sales for a while but didn't have to. Betty continued to work and save for her dream of studying dance at a more serious level in New York City.

The protective nature of Hortense went beyond sheltering the children from William's drinking, and surfaced in other areas as well. One such area centered around Betty's desire to study dance in New York. When Betty broached the subject, Hortense responded that Betty could not go until she turned twenty. Betty had lived with Hortense long enough to know when something was non-negotiable — this was one such time. Since she realized that her mother would not budge, and that the bond between them was too strong for her to simply run away and ignore her mother's directive, Betty pushed for a compromise. Hortense acquiesced to the idea of Betty studying dance at the Bennington School of Dance for two years before turning twenty. Hortense probably felt this was a safe alternative since the school was not in New York, and the school was more of a summer institute than a full-fledged school. Betty viewed it as professional training, while Hortense was more apt to have likened Bennington to summer camp.

After high school graduation, Betty did attend the Bennington School of Dance in Vermont. She vividly recalls the beauty of the area and has described the wildlife, the bright fall colors of the leaves, and the trout in the streams. Betty simply enjoyed every aspect of Bennington. Above all, she loved being able to dance eight hours a day with no outside interferences. While at the school, Betty studied with a number of well known dancers and choreographers including Louis Horst, Jose Limon, Hanya Holm, and Anna Sokolow.

Betty was a part of the Anna Sokolow group — various instructors would select students to work with and teach their routines to. Betty's Bennington life was one of taking classes all day and rehearsing with the Sokolow group in the evenings. Betty soon discovered that serious dancing is extremely strenuous work. She and her best friend, Natalie Harris, had no trouble walking upstairs to eat dinner but getting down was a different story! Their legs were so tired from dancing that their muscles knotted up and their knees refused to flex (fairly amusing for a girl who once designed a costume to hide the fact that her knees weren't straight). Betty and Natalie resorted to sliding down the stairs one at a time. Despite the pain, Betty would not have traded it for the world.

In addition to the physical rigor of dance, Betty was introduced to some of the more technical aspects of the art while at Bennington. One such aspect was dance notation. Betty had always been able to write down instructions in English or by drawing simple stick figures and arrows. For the life of her, she just couldn't grasp dance notation. The technical aspect was not what had drawn Betty to dance, she just wanted the freedom of expression. In her words, "oh, it was

Teens and Early Adulthood

terrible stuff for a booby who wanted only to soar, and who didn't care a fig for recording how she'd done it."[4]

Despite the frustration, Betty loved the discipline. Perhaps this stemmed from her strict upbringing and the discipline instilled in her by her mother. Regardless, Betty was drawn to the strictest of the disciplinarians at Bennington — Martha Graham. From the moment they met, Betty was mesmerized by Martha Graham, and idolized her from day one. Martha Graham made quite an impression indeed. According to Mrs. Ford,

> It's almost impossible to describe the impression made by Martha Graham on a girl who came to her straight out of high school. I worshiped her as a goddess. She was a tough disciplinarian; believe me, if you got her knee in your back when you weren't sitting up straight enough during an exercise, you never forgot it. But as I've said before, I admired that kind of strictness.[5]

This was all in Betty's first summer at Bennington.

Upon returning to Grand Rapids, Betty was very active in the community doing charity work and socializing with her friends. There were any number of football games and dances on the weekends. She also continued to model and teach dance. What she was really doing was biding her time until she could return to Bennington. She did have a year to get into better shape for the rigors of the dance school and had time to reflect on what the upcoming summer would bring. One thing was certain, Betty wanted to work with Martha Graham.

Betty returned for her second summer at Bennington and has revealed little of the experience. Perhaps this is because it was no longer new and exciting. She knew what to expect and approached the second year more seriously. What is certain is that the second summer at Bennington allowed Betty to establish closer ties to her idol, Martha Graham.

Martha's forte was modern dance. While many people failed to understand the beauty of this relatively new form — a 1934 Vermont newspaper ran the headline "Bennington Campus Seethes with Women Who Jump in Odd Fashion," in response to some of Graham's routines — Betty loved it. She had not lost the taste for the fluidity that she had acquired as a younger dancer. To her, modern dance allowed for a freedom of expression and release that she had not found with other forms. Watching Martha Graham in action simply reinforced her view of modern dance. She wanted to continue to study with Graham but didn't have the courage to ask during the second year at Bennington.

In the fall, after her return from Bennington, Betty noticed that Martha Graham and her dancing troupe, the Graham Crackers, were giving a concert in Ann Arbor. On her home turf, Betty felt much more at ease and surprised herself by asking if she could go to New York to study with Ms. Graham. Caught up in the exhilaration of the performance, the request was more of a blurted utterance, "If I come to New York, can I be at your school?" Ms. Graham said, "yes."

Betty Bloomer was now twenty — the age agreed upon by she and her mother — and about to leave the comforts of Grand Rapids to live out her childhood dream of studying dance in New York City.

Betty and Hortense drove East to meet Betty's roommate and friend from Bennington, Natalie Harris. Natalie had also been accepted into Martha Graham's fold, and the two were going to live together in the city and study with one another at the Graham studio. Initially, Natalie had found them a place in Greenwich village but Hortense took one look at the house and said that it simply wouldn't do. Hortense had heard about "the village" and didn't want Betty to have anything to do with that colorful world. Hortense favored the Barbizon Hotel for Women — much more conservative and safe surroundings. Betty and Natalie persuaded Hortense to compromise on an apartment in the Chelsea neighborhood off of Sixth Avenue that was within walking distance of the Graham studio. It wasn't the village, but it wasn't the Barbizon.

Betty paid for her classes by working during the day (and taking classes at night). Her time spent as a model in Grand Rapids paid off and she eventually landed a job with the Powers agency, a big name in the modeling world. She got the job despite a rather awkward introduction to John Robert Powers, the owner of the agency. There were a number of women in his outer office applying for work but he settled on Betty and called her into his office. After having her stand up to see how tall she was, he asked her to lift up her dress so he could see her legs. Betty obliged by lifting her dress up about two inches whereupon he told her he wanted to see her legs, not her knees. Betty was torn between the desperate need to work and her modest upbringing and her mother's harsh warnings about New York men. The need to work won out and she hiked up her dress while glaring at Mr. Powers who was probably trying not to laugh at the situation. He told her that her legs were a bit on the heavy side but would do. This was her introduction into the world of New York modeling.

Money was still tight and both Natalie and Betty lived frugally and were thrilled when any of the hometown crowd showed up at their door offering to take them out. Dinner and dancing was a treat that Betty couldn't really afford on her budget. Being able to go out on the town on someone else's tab allowed Betty to enjoy the New York she had envisioned.

Apparently there were a lot of old flames and acquaintances dropping by because Betty's social life soon began to get in the way of her dancing. She loved the New York lifestyle and thought that she could handle both the dancing and the partying — she was wrong. Martha Graham began to notice that Betty was dragging in rehearsals and that the nightlife was beginning to take its toll. She and Betty began to talk about it. Martha told Betty that she had natural ability and had a future if she were willing to give everything else up. Betty replied that she wanted both, to which Martha replied, "You can't carouse and be a dancer too."[6]

Betty did settle down, somewhat, and began to apply herself to dancing. She decided to make whatever sacrifices were necessary in order for her to make it as a dancer. Unfortunately, Betty never made it out of the "B" group. Nat Harris managed to make it into the main troupe, but Betty did not. Even though she was not in the main group, the auxiliary group got to perform at Carnegie Hall, which thrilled Betty to no end. Performing in that prestigious venue made Betty feel as if she had made it as a dancer. Realistically, however, she was beginning to realize that she did not have what it took to be a professional dancer. Nevertheless, she persevered.

The turning point in Betty's New York adventure came when her mother came to stay for a two week visit. Hortense became worried when she realized that Betty loved the New York lifestyle and was on the verge of never returning home to Grand Rapids. Moreover, Hortense never imagined that Betty would continue to take her dancing so seriously. During her stay, Hortense made every effort to talk up the merits of Grand Rapids, to bring up old friends, and to try and make Betty feel homesick. It didn't work. Finally, in desperation, Hortense asked Betty to humor her by returning to Grand Rapids for a six month trial period. Hortense proposed that if, after six months, Betty wanted to return to New York, she would have Hortense's blessing and would never hear another word about it. To appease her mother, Betty agreed. Betty went to Martha Graham and told her about the arrangement whereupon Martha Graham told Betty that she too, thought it was a good idea. Ms. Graham had seen many dancers come and go, and she realized that, perhaps, Betty might be better off taking some time to evaluate her priorities. With that, Betty's stay in New York came to an end. Betty Bloomer returned to Grand Rapids.

EARLY ADULTHOOD

Betty did not lose touch with New York. Upon returning home, Betty supported herself by working at Herpolsheimers' Department store as a fashion co-ordinator. In addition to organizing fashion shows and window displays, Betty was often asked to go to New York to place orders. She also maintained contact with the art of dancing and became her own version of Martha Graham. When not working, Betty taught dance lessons for children. Betty also started her own dance company and introduced religious dance to the city of Grand Rapids. Betty did all of the choreography and taught the numbers to the dancers in her group. On one occasion, the troupe even performed a number called "Three Parables" in a local Baptist church, the Fountain Street Baptist Church. The group took their dancing as seriously as their founder, Elizabeth Bloomer. When not working at Herpolscheimer's, teaching dance to children, or working with her own dance company, Betty found time to work for her old mentor, Calla Travis, teaching modern dance at the Travis studio. Before she knew it, the six month trial period was over. She actually enjoyed the work she was doing and was able to go out at night without feeling guilty about neglecting her art. Despite being away from the city, Betty did manage to continue to lead an active social life.

Betty was often wined and dined by local bachelors but she never felt any particular attraction to any of them. To her, they all tended to be a bit too "stuffy." Nevertheless, Betty almost made the mistake of marrying a lawyer from Petoskey, Michigan. Her brother Bill and his wife were living there and invited Betty up for a visit. Once in Petoskey, Bill and his wife introduced Betty to one of their friends — the lawyer. He played such a meaningless role in her life that Betty doesn't even mention him by name in her autobiography. In any case, theirs was a whirlwind romance. By the time Betty left Petoskey, she had met his family, and they had even gone out and bought an engagement ring. This seemed like the thing to do at the time ... her friends were all getting married, and the mood seemed right while she was visiting in Petoskey. When he came calling in Grand Rapids, everything changed.

Her "fiancé" came to visit and they went out with a group of Betty's friends. Never one of the reserved types, she and her friends tended to laugh, have fun, and carry on for hours. This particular evening, they didn't return until roughly 4:00 a.m. The lawyer was apparently not amused and got into a somewhat heated debate with Betty about how things would be when they were married. When she pressed the issue, he responded that they would discuss it in the morning. Not to be dismissed, and all too aware that this was not the man for her, Betty replied that a morning discussion would not be necessary and that the "engagement" was over. She handed back the ring, and that was the end of the lawyer from Petoskey. He ended up being just another gentleman who was too stuffy for Betty's tastes. It seems that most young men were not up to her standards — most of them, that is, except a young man named Bill Warren.

Betty had known Bill for years and had actually dated him when they were younger. This was the same young man who had escorted Betty to her first dance when she was twelve. The Bill of her youth was undependable and liked a good time. She enjoyed the fun aspect but her mother had taught her to demand certain treatment — something the younger Bill was ill-equipped to provide. At one point, the young Betty Bloomer had told Bill Warren to get lost and never call her again. This time around, however, Betty found him to be more attractive and fun than she had in their earlier days. He was blond, athletic, and a very good dancer. In Betty's words, "he wasn't a bit stuffy." Betty and Bill became a couple and began to see more and more of each other. Unfortunately, her mother was not nearly as enthusiastic about Bill as Betty was.

This created something of a problem since Betty had earlier decided to give up her apartment and live with Hortense and Betty's step-father, Arthur Godwin. Since both Mr. and Mrs. Godwin frowned upon Betty having anything to do with Bill Warren, she had to sneak out of the house or lie about who she was seeing in order to avoid the inevitable confrontation with her mother. Eventually, things got too serious between Betty and Bill for them to hide their relationship any longer. Early in 1942, Bill and Betty announced their engagement — they were married in the spring. Despite showing little enthusiasm towards the young Mr. Warren, Hortense and Arthur Godwin appear to have come around once the engagement was announced. In fact, Betty and Bill were married in the Godwin's living room and the reception was held in the garden.

While Bill seemed like a fun person to be with, it soon became apparent that he wasn't suited to being the perfect mate Betty had envisioned. In fact, Bill Warren appears to have been a person in search of himself. This constant search kept him moving from town to town and job to job — always with Betty in tow. When they were first married, Bill was an insurance salesman but he soon quit that profession in order to become a furniture dealer. That too was short lived. In the next three years, Bill tried a variety of jobs but nothing ever seemed to work out.

Whenever the two could manage to stay put for any period of time, Bill would spend more time at the bar than at home. Betty often felt disappointed when, after she took the time to cook him a nice dinner, he would call and ask her to join him for drinks. According to biographer, Chris Chase, "she (Betty) said all of the fun that they'd had, going out to bars and drinking and being with friends was fine before she was married but then, after they were married, he would call her up at 10:00 at night and tell her he was down at the bar having a few drinks. He would ask her to join them and that they'd go out to dinner afterward."[7] In Bill's mind there was nothing wrong with joining the guys from work for a few drinks and then inviting Betty to join them for dinner. After all, she seemed to like it when they were dating. For Betty, however, what was fun while they were dating was something less than tolerable once they were married. There was an obvious difference between dating and marriage that her husband failed to notice.

Even though Bill was not the perfect mate, Betty did her very best to be the perfect wife and to make the marriage a success. She took on different jobs as Bill moved them around the Midwest and the East Coast. She worked in department stores, taught dance, and even worked for a brief time on the production line in a frozen food factory sorting and packaging produce. She even hunted for food on occasion (she once pulled out a 20 gauge shotgun and bagged one of the many rabbits that hopped around their home while they lived in Maumee, Ohio). Betty even did her best to keep up appearances and act as if she and Bill were happy. She never complained publicly and made every effort to present herself as the young, happy, wife.

Despite her efforts to make the marriage a success, things never truly worked out between Betty and Bill Warren. She had always wanted a husband who would stay at home and provide stability — this, of course, stemming from her disappointment with her own father's frequent absences. Bill could not live up to these expectations and never really found himself as either an individual or a partner in marriage. Needless to say, Betty was not happy and found married life to be a big disappointment. According to her brother, Bill Bloomer, "it was not as meaningful as she would have liked."[8]

After three years of just getting by and pretending that theirs was a good marriage, Betty finally got angry enough to put an end to the sham. While Bill was away on a sales trip she began to draft a letter asking Bill to not bother coming home when his job was finished and that she was sending his things to his parents. As she was about to send the letter, a call came from Bill's boss informing Betty that Bill had become very ill while in Boston. In fact, it seems as if his many years of drinking had come back to haunt him — he had slipped into a diabetic coma and wasn't expected to live. Betty flew to Boston immediately.

When Betty arrived she found that Bill had suffered partial paralysis in his face and that he was in very bad shape. She began to take classes to learn how to give Bill the daily insulin shots that he would require and decided that, despite the fact that she didn't love him anymore, she would remain with him in order to take care of him. To defray some of the costs of the extended stay in Boston, Betty stayed with friends. Her time in Boston was spent entirely by Bill's side at the hospital. After six weeks, Bill's father came to take them all back to Grand Rapids. Bill was still in very bad shape and had to be transported by ambulance to the train. He was still bed ridden and they weren't sure how long he would remain alive.

Back in Grand Rapids, the Warrens rented a hospital bed so that Bill could stay at home while the family provided care. Betty went back to work at Herpolsheimer's and would simply shuffle back and forth between work and the Warren's home where she would attend to Bill. By this time, doctors had informed the family that Bill would most likely never walk again. Betty was devastated and felt as if her whole life lay before her — and she didn't like what she saw. She was twenty-seven years old and was to be defined by her ability to work hard and provide care for a man that she didn't really love. To her credit, Betty remained by Bill's side for the next two years in order to take care of him.

After roughly two years of being bed-ridden and pretty much written off, Bill Warren experienced a miraculous recovery. Not only did the paralysis go away, but he was able to get out of bed and could take care of himself. He had made a complete recovery and even went back to work. This made it possible for Betty to, in good conscience, resume the separation she had begun two years earlier with the letter she never sent to Bill. Betty went to see a divorce attorney and began the process of legal separation. Bill was aware of the fact that the marriage was broken, too. He didn't contest the divorce and, in order to make it legal, gave Betty one dollar as a divorce settlement. For Betty, it was time to move on and in her words the whole episode was a "five year misunderstanding." The year was 1947 and Betty was on her own.

Betty knew that she had to find meaningful work and that she would be on her own from now on. Since most of her experience was in fashion (from modeling in New York and working as the fashion coordinator at Herpolsheimer's), she thought that her fortunes most likely lay in that field. To this end, she even considered a move to Rio de Janeiro, which was a major fashion center at the time. Regardless of what she did do, she was fairly certain about what she was not going to do — get married again. Between her experience with the lawyer in Petoskey and her "five year misunderstanding" with Bill Warren, Betty had pretty much determined that serious commitment and a long-term relationship were not for her. She had not yet met Gerald R. Ford!

IMPORTANT HIGHLIGHTS

One of the most important things to focus on from Betty's teenage years and early adulthood is her ability to socialize. From the Good Cheers, her time in New York, and playing the field in Grand Rapids upon her return, Betty gained the ability to function in social settings. Betty simply loved parties! As first lady, this skill would be of the utmost importance. Most people fail to realize the importance that the hostess role plays in presidential success. When foreign dignitaries or even political opponents come to the White House, there is an opportunity for the president to make allegiances and to gain political advantages. A strategically planned and well-executed party can go a long way to disarm even the most ardent foes. Moreover, the first lady is expected to travel abroad and serve as a symbolic extension of our government. First ladies such as Jackie Kennedy were able to smooth over relations with nations (in her case France) in ways that their husbands were not. Betty's ability to engage everyone around her stemmed largely from her earlier years and was a tremendous asset. This period also illustrates Betty Ford's deep sense of loyalty and commitment. That she was willing to stay with a man she didn't love when he was in need of help points to the fact that she could place the welfare of others above her own. Taking care of others at her own expense would later come to haunt her.

Chapter 3

GERALD R. FORD, JR.

Gerald R. Ford, Jr. was born Leslie L. King, Jr. on July 14, 1913 in Omaha, Nebraska to Leslie Lynch King and Dorothy (Gardner) King. His parents had a very tumultuous relationship and, from many accounts, the elder Leslie King was an abusive husband. By 1915, when the young Gerald Ford (still named Leslie King, Jr.) was only two years old, his parents divorced and Dorothy moved to Grand Rapids to live with her family.

In Grand Rapids, Dorothy met and fell in love with a young paint salesman named Gerald R. Ford. The two were married and lived in a rented apartment on Madison Avenue in Grand Rapids. Over time, Gerald Ford became more and more successful as a salesman and even branched out into other ventures. Along the way, he bought his growing family a home on Rosewood Avenue and formally adopted his stepson Leslie. With the adoption came a new name — Gerald R. Ford, Jr. — Jerry Ford. After all, the elder Gerald Ford was really the only father that young Jerry had ever known. In fact, Jerry only met his biological father once — for a brief time one afternoon in his teens. The meeting left Jerry with the impression that his biological father was a carefree, well-to-do man who really cared little, if anything, about his first born son.

Jerry inherited his biological father's hot temper and had to learn how to control his urges to lash out. His mother, Dorothy, was instrumental in helping the young boy to overcome his problems with anger and a hot temper. Like Betty Bloomer's mother, Hortense, Dorothy was a strict disciplinarian and demanded certain things of her offspring. She simply would not tolerate a hotheaded son that came unglued at every turn. Dorothy apparently tried everything from ridiculing Jerry and telling him how stupid he looked every time he got angry to physically twisting his ear. Perhaps the most effective technique Dorothy used to break Jerry of his anger problem was her habit of sending him to his room and ordering him to stay there until he was ready to come downstairs and rationally discuss whatever problem he might have been having. In other words, Dorothy made Jerry take what we refer to today as "a time out." Eventually, Dorothy was able to teach Jerry how to control his temper and as an adult he is often remembered for his even manner and ability to keep things in check through difficult times.

Both Dorothy and her husband Gerald were strict with the children but also made them feel extremely loved. Jerry never once doubted that either one of his parents would do anything for him and his siblings. The strict discipline and undying love were combined to instill in the children three primary traits — tell the truth, work hard, and never show up late for dinner. As an adult, Jerry would always adhere to the first two but would often have problems with the third (much to Betty's chagrin).

His parents' love and insistence on honesty and integrity aided young Gerald in other ways. He became very perceptive and in tune with the needs and desires of other people. As early as the seventh grade, he recognized the deep emotions that can arise from rivalries — whether the rivalry be in sports, romance, or even politics. He realized that intense rivalry had set many of his classmates apart to the point of actual dislike. As a seventh grader, he developed a philosophy that would sustain him for the rest of his life and was an approach that certainly lended itself to a successful career in politics — he decided that every person has more good qualities than bad and that by understanding and emphasizing the good points in others, he could get along much better.

In his words, "hating or even disliking people because of their bad qualities, it seemed to me, was a waste of time."[1]

Gerald Ford was groomed to be a well rounded individual by his parents who emphasized grades, athletics, and part-time employment. They firmly believed that athletics helped to build a boy's character and instilled in an individual a sense of teamwork. To this end, they pushed young Gerald to participate in sports from an early age. He did so eagerly and was very good at most sports that he tried — he was particularly good at football where he played center in both high school and college. They also pushed him to excel academically — something that came less naturally than his sports proficiency. Gerald always did very well in history, government and math. Courses such as Latin, chemistry, and other science courses proved to be much more difficult. In the more trying courses, Gerald had to work very hard in order to pull down average grades. The hard work paid off as the average grades were balanced out by the exceptional grades in other classes to the point that he was named to the National Honor Society by the end of his junior year of high school. Throughout high school, at the insistence of his parents, Gerald held down numerous part-time jobs in addition to spending hours studying and playing sports. He was already being groomed for the long hours that he would later spend in politics.

After high school, he attended the University of Michigan on scholarship where he majored in economics and political science. His eventual goal was to become an attorney. Despite his gift for athletics, his scholarship was not for sports, it was the South High "bookstore scholarship," which was the creation of the school principal, Arthur Krause. It seems that the one and only recipient of the "bookstore scholarship" was Gerald Ford — the person for whom Krause had created the scholarship. By doing so, Krause had provided Ford with his first year's tuition but nothing else. The family was strapped financially and Gerald had to earn his living expenses and money for school supplies. Throughout college, Ford worked at everything from waiting tables and cleaning up the cafeteria to working in a paint factory. Ford even donated blood for cash at the university hospital — he was determined to stay in school and get an education despite the tremendous financial barriers in his way.

Over time, Gerald Ford developed into a tremendously gifted athlete and would later use his athleticism to both his academic and political advantage. It was during his time at the University of Michigan that he began to solidify his reputation around Grand Rapids and to establish firm name recognition which is very important in politics — he was the local football hero from South High and many people in Grand Rapids were familiar with the name of Gerald Ford. Moreover, U of M football is enormously popular in the state of Michigan, and Gerald Ford was one of the team's few bright spots during a losing season his senior year. Because of his athletic reputation and instant name recognition, Betty Bloomer had heard of Jerry Ford before they ever really met. In fact, everybody in Grand Rapids knew who he was. According to one of Betty's friends, Lillian Fisher, "when we were teenagers, he was our football hero, I mean it was like, Gary Cooper and Jerry Ford."[2] He was that popular!

Upon graduation, Ford was approached by two professional football teams (the Lions and Packers) but he rejected them both. He felt that a career in professional football would not lead him anywhere. Instead of playing professional football, Ford decided to accept an offer to serve as a boxing coach and assistant football coach at Yale. After all, Ford hoped to become an attorney and he figured that Yale law school was one of the best. Eventually Ford was admitted to the Yale School of Law and he graduated in the top 25 percent of his class. Along the way, Ford was given a taste for politics when he worked for a brief time on the presidential campaign of Wendell Wilkie.

Ford returned to Michigan and worked as an attorney prior to joining the U.S. Navy in 1942. His initial assignment was as a physical fitness instructor at flight school in North Carolina and he felt somewhat slighted. He had joined the navy to help out in the war, not to serve in a non-combat capacity. He wrote letters to everyone he knew in a desperate effort to be assigned a position on a combat ship. His letter writing campaign paid off when he was assigned to the light aircraft carrier U.S.S. Monterey in 1943. On the Monterey, Ford saw a great deal of action and engaged in many battles. Ford served in the South Pacific until the U.S.S. Monterey was damaged during a 1944 storm. Ironically, despite the many firefights and missions carried out by the Monterey, it was during this 1944 typhoon in the Philippine Sea that Ford came the closest to death. According to him, the night of the storm "was pure hell."[3] The storm resulted in a tremendous loss of life by sinking other ships and caused crippling damage to the Monterey. With the ship out of commission, Ford spent the remainder of his military time on dry land — until 1946 when he was discharged.

Upon returning to Grand Rapids, Ford once again practiced law. However, his overseas experience had given him a more international outlook than he had enjoyed in his youth and he decided that isolationism was not an appropriate course for our country. The Wilkie experience had him thinking in political terms, after all. With the encouragement of his stepfather and local political leaders, Ford set out to challenge the isolationist incumbent Bartel Jonkman for the Republican nomination for the U.S. House of Representatives in Michigan's fifth district. Defeating Jonkman in the 1948 election would be no small task and the only things that young Ford had going for him were his name, Jonkman's overconfidence as a seemingly unbeatable incumbent in a safe district, and the element of surprise. All of Ford's strategists maintained that they needed to keep his candidacy a secret until the last possible moment so that Jonkman could not mobilize for a counter-attack. This meant keeping his candidacy a secret from the woman he had been dating for about six months — Betty Warren.

Ford had been back in Grand Rapids for quite some time after the war and was active in both his law career and in many various civic activities. There was almost no cause he would not support and he became a "compulsive joiner." He was active in the Red Cross, the American Legion, the local cancer drive, Family Services, and the Boy Scouts, among others. It was during his work with the local cancer drive that he began to feel like his diminishing social life was a potential problem. All of his brothers were married, and his mother's continuous reminder that he was in his mid-thirties with no signs of settling down began to hit home. One evening he was with his friends, Peg and Frank Newman, helping to plan the cancer drive when he asked whether either of them knew of anyone in town that a bachelor his age might be able to date. Betty happened to be one of Peg's best friends so her name came up instantly. Being somewhat shy, Jerry had Peg call her.

Peg asked Betty if she wouldn't mind meeting Jerry for a drink — Betty said "no." Betty was working and felt that taking time away would be a bad idea. After all, she had to get up early and didn't want to go to work dragging the next day. Jerry took the phone away from Peg and began to give Betty a big song and dance about how going out with him for a couple of drinks would actually be refreshing for her and that she would feel better at work the next day. She continued to refuse and reminded him that she was still married and that it wouldn't look too good for them to be seen together. As a lawyer, couldn't he understand that? According to him, he did understand but still wasn't going to give up. He continued with his theory that going out would be refreshing until she finally caved in and agreed to meet him. They differ as to whether they agreed to meet for an hour or so (his version) or a mere twenty minutes (her version). Regardless of the specific agreement, they agreed to meet for a brief time that evening and this was how their relationship began. At the time, he wasn't aware that someone special had come into his life but she felt something. Despite the fact that she had sworn off serious relationships, she couldn't help but wonder whether there were some possibilities. In her words, "I can't say love at first sight but it certainly was I wonder if, maybe, it wouldn't work if we got together."[4]

He was recently coming off of a long-term relationship and her divorce was not yet final. Needless to say, neither one was looking for a serious relationship. In fact, they both agreed to take things lightly and to not take each other seriously. Despite their intentions, they got along famously and began to see more and more of one another. They even ran into Betty's mother and stepfather one evening outside of the movie theater. Jerry and Betty were in line for tickets and Hortense and Mr. Godwin were coming out after viewing an earlier show. Since Betty was not yet officially divorced, Hortense, being the strict proprietarian that she was, was somewhat shocked. She had nothing against Jerry, but Betty was a married woman. Betty did the only proper thing she could which was to introduce everyone.

Once Betty's divorce was final, Jerry and Betty continued to see quite a bit of one another but they maintained their position that it wasn't to become too serious. They also dated other people but preferred each other's company. At one point, despite the agreement that things be kept at a friendly, social level, Jerry showed some signs of jealousy. He arrived at Betty's apartment one evening to find that there were a few young men already there. Everyone was drinking and carrying on — except for Jerry who simply sat on the sofa and cooly opened up the newspaper, without saying a word. After some time, two of the young men felt that the tension was too high and left. One gentleman was willing to sit and wait Jerry out. The two were at a stand-off and finally Betty had witnessed enough. She declared that, since she had to work the next day, she was going to bed and that the two of them would have to go home. They both left in silence — Jerry hadn't spoken the entire time he was in the apartment. Outside, Jerry asked the young man what his intentions were towards Betty. When the man replied that he was very interested, Jerry responded that he just wanted to know. Neither knew that Betty's window was open and that she could hear every word. While she was somewhat taken aback by Jerry's forward actions and was under the impression that they weren't supposed to be getting serious, her recollection of the event reveals that she was secretly pleased.

According to Betty, her true interest in Jerry was put to the test when the snows came and she had to learn to ski. Jerry had done quite a bit of skiing in law school and back East and liked to go skiing every weekend when the weather permitted. He convinced her to give it a try. Jerry and Betty went shopping for clothes and ski equipment and headed up north to spend the weekend with a group of friends. Jerry taught her the basics and then left her to fend for herself while he did some real skiing. Apparently this didn't upset Betty too much since they began to go north for skiing weekends almost all of the time during the winter and Betty began to seriously question the ground rules of their relationship. She was falling in love and was fearful that the sentiment wouldn't be returned — even worse, she feared that getting serious might drive Jerry away.

The ultimate test of their relationship came over the Christmas holidays of 1947. Jerry left for Sun Valley, Idaho on a skiing trip that would keep him away for three weeks. Because of work, Betty was not able to go with him. This was the first time that they had been apart for an extended period of time since they had begun dating and Betty knew that she would miss him. She was even feeling a little jealous knowing that he would have a good time and that women seemed to always follow him around. To ensure that he remembered her, Betty put together a little care package for his trip comprised of little gifts and trinkets that would remind him of her. Included in the stocking that she had one of the seamstresses from Herpolsheimer's create (it was a Christmas trip) were a pair of dark glasses with blinders on them to keep his attention focused on skiing, a toy train since he was going to Sun Valley by rail, and a pipe lighter with the personal engraving "to the light of my life." Betty was somewhat afraid of sticking her neck out with the inscription, but she did it anyway and then tucked the lighter into the toe of the stocking.

Gerald R. Ford, Jr. 31

While he was gone, Betty did her best to keep busy and to keep her mind off of Jerry — it didn't work. It seems that Jerry missed her too because he wrote to her everyday. Moreover, he bought her a handcrafted belt which he presented to her when he got back to Grand Rapids. The belt was not important, the significance of the gift was. One of his friends found out about the seemingly innocuous present and responded by stating, "Jerry Ford actually gave a present to a *girl*? This must be serious."[5] The friend was correct. Despite their initial agreement to keep things light and to not get too serious about one another, Betty and Jerry were deeply in love. In February of 1947, a mere six months after they began dating, Jerry asked Betty to marry him and she eagerly accepted.

When Jerry proposed, he said they couldn't get married until the fall but he neglected to tell Betty why. She would soon find out that the "why" was he was planning a run for Congress. She was initially hurt that she had to find out about his political aspirations from the newspaper rather than from him. This is certainly understandable but she also admits that if she had known that he was going to be in politics, rather than being the stable career minded attorney she envisioned, it might have scared her off. Despite finding out from third party sources, Betty was crazy about Jerry and wasn't going to hold something like this against him for long. Instead she decided to help out in any way she could. One way was to wait on announcing their engagement. Michigan's fifth district was comprised of many strict Dutch conservatives who might frown on their congressman dating a divorcee who had also been a dancer in New York. His strategists felt that their engagement had to be kept a secret until after the critical primary election against Jonkman — the general election was meaningless. Ford had to agree with his advisors and Betty gamely agreed to keep things quiet. Rather than becoming a political liability, Betty proved herself to be quite an asset. She jumped right in and helped with his campaign and also got some of the models from Herpolsheimer's, her dancing friends, and anyone she could corral to assist with the effort. There was an excitement in the air and everyone involved got wrapped up in the "Ford for Congress" movement. While Betty was thoroughly invested in Jerry's cause, the initial excitement eventually led to the realization of what her life was about to look like.

Despite her childhood decision to marry a man who would be a permanent household fixture, Jerry Ford was married to his work and would be required to be away quite often. The night of the primary — that Jerry won — turned into a planning session for the next round (Betty had thought they could finally plan for the wedding). On the eve of their wedding rehearsal dinner, Jerry showed up for cocktails and then left to make a speech when the rest of the family went in to eat. Betty was left at the head of the table all alone until the minister took pity upon her and moved into the groom's spot at the table (Jerry did return in time for dessert). Finally, on the very day of their wedding, October 15, 1948, Jerry was late in arriving because he was out campaigning. Betty later told him that if he hadn't shown up, she would have married someone else. She was kidding of course — she loved him and his frequent absences would not change that.

Even their honeymoon was centered around politics. Rather than take time away and do traditional honeymoon activities, the Fords went to Ann Arbor for a party at the Town Club followed by attendance at a University of Michigan football game the next day. The game was followed by a trip to Owosso for a political rally being held by Republican presidential hopeful, Thomas Dewey. Betty wasn't interested in hearing Dewey at all, but they stayed until the very end anyway. Then, it was off to Detroit where Jerry spent time gathering up newspapers and taking in the political environment. They returned to Ann Arbor where Jerry had some meetings with university faculty and then they headed home — a truly romantic affair. Once they arrived home, Betty had envisioned herself as the happy homemaker in an evening gown waiting to share a nice home-cooked meal with her new husband. This was the same type of vision she had in mind when married to Bill Warren. Before they even hit the Grand Rapids city limits, Jerry informed Betty that he had an important political meeting that evening and wondered whether she might be willing to fix him a sandwich and some soup. Once again, she had found a man who was going to be away quite often. It didn't matter, she loved him dearly and would take him as he was. The Fords were a couple, Jerry was the consummate politician, and together they were about to go to Washington.

IMPORTANT HIGHLIGHTS

The most significant points from the preceding section have to do with Jerry's ambition and Betty's devotion to her husband and willingness, once again, to fall in love with a man who would be away from home. Despite her childhood desire to never marry a man who would be gone often, it was clear that this was the very type of man she was attracted to. When her engagement was prefaced by Jerry telling her there was something he had to do — without telling her what that was — and her wedding dinner being interrupted by campaigning, Betty was fully aware of what her future life might look like. Simply put, Gerald Ford was a political animal and anyone who wanted to be around him would have to accept that. Betty would have to accept the fact that she might be alone for much of the time. This could have been viewed as nothing but a big negative, however, Betty realized that there were also some positives involved. She realized that she could play a large role in helping Jerry with his plans and that, together, they could forge a partnership. In this role, Betty could be a valuable asset and could be a participant in Jerry's life rather than just a part-time observer. It was this partnership that would enable Gerald Ford to have a long and hugely successful political career and would, in many ways, form the core of Betty's future identity.

Chapter 4

NEW JOB, NEW FAMILY

CONGRESS

When Betty and Jerry Ford left Grand Rapids for his first term as a U.S. Congressman, she didn't really know what to expect. It was a foregone conclusion that the quiet life with an established lawyer and the typical 1950's family would not be in her future. Knowing this did not necessarily prepare her for what lay ahead. Washington, D.C. and national politics is a far cry from Grand Rapids, Michigan and a district level campaign. Betty Ford was about to begin a new chapter in her life and, much to her dismay, was about to have an old chapter closed for her.

Shortly after arriving in Washington, Jerry and Betty were looking for an apartment when a call came from Jerry's family in Grand Rapids informing Betty that her mother was very ill in a Florida hospital. Betty got on the first plane out of Washington and should have arrived in Florida at a reasonable hour. Unfortunately, there were mechanical problems and her flight was severely delayed. After several hours, Betty made it down the ramp in Florida at 9:00 p.m. where her stepfather was waiting for her — Hortense had died of cerebral hemorrhaging at 6:00. Betty tried to convince herself and her step-father that it was for the best and that her passing was a blessing because Hortense would not have like to have lived a restricted life had she survived the hemorrhaging. The damage was done and it would have been hard on Hortense to try and live as a shadow of her former self. Despite convincing themselves that her ultimate passing was for the best, they felt a sense of great loss. The loss was especially hard on Betty who was extremely close to her mother. Betty was now expected to enter into a new marriage, in a new and stressful city with new rules, and move forward without the aid of her role model, mentor, and confidant.

The Fords eventually managed to find a small one-bedroom apartment in Georgetown. For the time being, the apartment at 2500 Q Street would meet their needs adequately. They didn't have any children and the two of them didn't need a whole lot of space. Even with there being only two people, they had a woman come in to do housekeeping for them. In the early days, Betty probably needed to have someone take care of the house because she had a steep learning curve to overcome when it came to government, politics, and life in Washington. Much of her time was spent learning the ropes!

Betty spent time going to sessions of the Supreme Court, observing house and senate debates, and she even took time to observe the inner workings of the committee system. In short, Betty was getting a first hand education in American government. There was much that she hadn't known, and she was fairly impressed with the power wielded by some of the more established members of Congress. She also learned, first hand, that it takes a thick skin to succeed in politics. Gerald Ford received numerous letters and postcards criticizing his actions. One example was a constituent who took exception to Jerry's posing with a local high school class when he could have been on the hill working. Betty took offense to this because she knew that her husband was a hard-working, conscientious man. Jerry told her to ignore it — this would become commonplace and she had better get used to it. There would never be a day when everyone was satisfied, and getting critical letters was simply a part of the political game. Moreover, in the case of the disgruntled constituent who felt that posing with a high school class was not work and got in the way of a congressperson's success on the hill, some people simply didn't understand how politics worked. In Jerry's case, posing with that high school class probably gained more votes — and thus more potential power — than being on the hill that particular day. This was work and posing with people in his district while performing constituent service was a big part of his job.

Betty assisted with constituent service too. She would often take guests on tours of Washington and serve as hostess during their visits. Over time, she got so used to visiting such sites as Mount Vernon, that she would simply take along a book and wait in the parking lot. She became a frequent guest of many a parking lot in the early years, but she was simply doing her part to help out in the political partnership. She also became active in many social groups such as the Congressional Club. The Club, comprised of congressional wives, wives of cabinet members, and the wives of Supreme Court justices, was a bipartisan group that engaged in a number of activities. The members played cards, helped out at the local Red Cross, learned foreign languages, and kept themselves busy in a wide range of areas. One activity that Betty frequented was the weekly book review. She truly enjoyed listening to what others had to say about current literature — until it was her turn to give a review. She was somewhat scared and asked a friend back in Grand Rapids what to do, what to read, and how to go about giving this review. Her experience with reviewing *Popcorn on the Ginza* allowed her to take a step towards becoming a better public speaker (something she would be very good at as a first lady). After doing the review, Betty even took a public speaking class so that she could do better in the future.

Her experience in the Congressional Club was very positive for Betty and made it possible for her to meet a large number of people and to become friends with a number of wives that she might not have otherwise met. Most of her new friends were Democrats (Jerry was Republican) since the sweeping tide in the most recent election didn't result in very many Republicans coming to Washington for the 81st Congress. Among her closest friends at the time were Abigail McCarthy and Muriel Humphrey. To this day, Betty remarks on the civility that was a part of politics and Congress back then. Congresspersons would berate each other on the floor of the House over issues, but would not ever let the attacks get personal. These same people could be found patting each other on the back over a job well done or a position well stated later on in the day. Politics was their job and they didn't let it spill over into their personal lives. She is somewhat disappointed that congresspersons in the new millennium seem to have lost their civility. Nevertheless, Betty made many good friends amongst "the enemy." She had a special respect for Lady Bird Johnson who made a special effort to include them as newcomers into the Washington fold. Betty felt she was a truly warm, friendly, outgoing person — a good role model to follow when she would later ascend into the office of first lady.

Another part of Jerry's job was attending social functions in both his home district and in Washington. During the early transition period for the couple, Jerry often attended social functions alone. Betty would run into some of the other congressional wives the next day and they would ask why she hadn't been in attendance. They saw Jerry, but they didn't see Betty. She would reply that she hadn't been invited; the invitation had been addressed to Representative Gerald R. Ford with no Mrs. attached. Apparently, not everyone in town knew that Jerry Ford, the newest member of the Michigan delegation, was married. There were enough of these awkward encounters with her friends from the Congressional Club that Betty finally decided that she needed to deal with the situation. After Betty had a little "chat" with Jerry about the situation, he went about the process of informing people around Washington that he was, in fact, not a bachelor. Joint invitations soon followed.

One cannot understate the importance of Betty's taking the time to observe the intricacies of Washington political life and to learn about protocol. Bureaucracies are generally driven by rules, procedures, culture, and tradition. In this sense, Washington and national politics is very bureaucratic. There is a higherarchical pecking order for senators and members of the House, and everything is done according to custom and tradition. The careers of many would-be politicians have been cut short because they inadvertently offended the wrong people by failing to follow protocol. Many laws and policies have failed to come to fruition because their sponsors had tripped over protocol. We have even experienced international tensions because one side or the other caused offense because of failure to recognize the proper protocol. In short, politics and protocol are intertwined. The time that Betty spent trying to "learn the ropes" was time well spent. By reading books (she even bought a book on when to wear gloves at tea), asking questions, and observing everything and everyone around her, Betty learned protocol. The long time that she and Jerry spent in Washington prior to entering the White House certainly helped Betty in her ability to always know the proper protocol for a given situation and to always be prepared.

Betty was becoming the perfect political wife — learning protocol, making friends with the right people, ushering around constituents, and even sharing her pancake recipe with the newspaper. This was good for Jerry who had decided that he wanted to one day become the Speaker of the House. It was also good for Betty but it simply wasn't fulfilling. She wanted more. What she wanted, was to have children. She still longed for the normal stay at home family existence that she had dreamed of her entire life. Even though it was fairly clear that Jerry would not be a stay at home dad, Betty wanted to have children and to be more of a stay at home mom. Besides, she was thirty years old and Jerry was thirty-five. The time to act was now.

After about six months of trying to have children with no success, Betty began to wonder if there was something wrong with Jerry. They went to the doctor only to find out that Jerry was fine, but Betty had a tipped uterus. The doctor proceeded to correct her problem and the Fords were on their way to starting a family. By the summer of 1949, roughly ten months after they were married, Betty Ford was pregnant and about to start the family that she always wanted.

The Ford Family

Betty spent much of her early pregnancy in Michigan instead of Washington because of the heat. Their apartment didn't have air conditioning and Washington can get quite hot in the summertime. Despite the fact that Betty had a very conventional aunt who felt that she needed to be by her husband's side at all times, her step-father and Jerry both made the decision that the aunt would be overruled and Betty would be staying in Michigan. The doctor was concerned with Betty's age and the potential for miscarriage and the family wasn't about to take any chances.

Betty actually stayed in Michigan, at her stepfather's lake-side cottage, until January of 1950. She stayed well past the hot part of summer and well into the coldest part of the winter. It was simply easier on her to live in a one-story home without stairs. Besides, by the time the heat ended, Jerry was back in session and couldn't take care of her anyway. Once the session ended, it was Christmastime and all of their friends and family were in Michigan anyway. It just made sense for Betty to stay out of Washington. Around the holidays, however, Betty began to get nervous. They hadn't really been married that long, what if Jerry didn't take to being a father? Was her spending too much time away detrimental to their marriage? She wanted to be with Jerry. Moreover, she firmly believed that she needed to be home and that, once there, she needed to have a son. She thought that there would be no doubt that Jerry would take to being the father of a boy.

It took them quite some time to find out whether their baby would be a boy or girl. Many of Betty's friends had delivered two weeks early — not Betty. It seemed as if her pregnancy went on and on, and would never end. At one point she was downtown shopping when an acquaintance asked her when she was due. Betty casually informed her that she was two weeks past the due date. When the woman told her that she had better go home and lay down, Betty told her she was trying to walk the baby out. No amount of walking seemed to work, however. Finally, her doctor asked if she'd like to come down the hospital and have her baby — she had gone dangerously long and he was ready to induce labor. Even that didn't seem to help right away. The doctor finally told Jerry to go home and that he'd call when the baby arrived. On March 14, 1950, Michael Gerald Ford was born. They had their baby boy which Betty accredited to God's will and Jerry attributed to fatherly genetics. They were both extremely happy and proud!

Betty had some help in raising Mike and in doing work around the house from a woman named Clara Powell. Clara was the daughter-in-law of the Fords first cleaning lady, Ida. Ida had left the Fords for a full-time job with a school and asked if it would be okay with the Fords if Clara took her place. Little did they know at the time that Clara would become one of the family and would be with them for many years. In his own biography, Gerald Ford remarked that Clara had played an integral role in their family and that it was common for him to remark that if Clara left them, he'd have to quit Congress. He emphasized that it was Clara who often served as the key player in times of family crisis and that "All of us loved her as one of us because she *was* one of us."[1] Betty jokingly referred to Clara as "the other woman." Mrs. Ford would later devote an entire chapter to Clara Powell in *The Times of My Life.*

By the time that Mike was about a year and a half, the family was still living in the apartment on Q street and it was getting hard for Clara to take care of him. The apartment was not on the first floor and every time Clara wanted to take Mike outside she had to go to the carriage room, get the carriage, manage to get Mike into the carriage, and then get herself and Mike (hopefully still in the carriage) onto the elevator. Mike was getting to the point that his climbing ability made it virtually impossible to keep him in one place. Moreover, he was close to walking and they wanted to live in a place where he could go outside and run around without too much worry. With that in mind, the Fords moved out of Georgetown into Fairfax Park in Virginia. They found a garden level apartment without many steps to accommodate Clara in her efforts to take care of Mike, and to make things easier on Betty who had suffered through a miscarriage a few months earlier. Jerry and Betty wanted to have a larger family and didn't want to take any unnecessary chances if Betty were to become pregnant again.

The Fords also had a modest two-family home in Grand Rapids that they had purchased so Jerry could stay in closer touch with his constituents. They felt that buying a two-family home would allow them the luxury of maintaining two residences without the exorbitant costs. They planned on living in one part of the house and renting out the other. While the thought was that Jerry would be spending more time there than the rest of the family, the entire bunch lived in Michigan for half of the year up through the time that Mike was in kindergarten.

Having a bottom story in Michigan and a garden level apartment in Virginia turned out to be a good idea because Betty did get pregnant again. Not to break tradition, she once again suffered through another very long pregnancy and ended up having to have the birth induced. The timing was such that Betty considered having the child on March 14 so that both children would share the same birthday. After further consideration, Betty decided a shared birthday would actually deprive each of their own special day. The Fords' second son, John Gardner (Jack), was born on March 16, 1952.

The two boys, despite being born close together and sharing the same astrological symbol (Pisces), were very different people. One was adventurous, the other cautious. One was neat, and the other was less than tidy. Betty has remarked that a person could draw a line down the center of their shared bedroom and have two very different worlds on either side — they were that opposite. In her words, "one side would look like a picture out of *Boy's Life* magazine, and the other side would look as if a bomb went off in a thrift shop."[2] The important thing to remember is that the Fords let them be who they were and did not really try to mold them into any one type of child or person. Betty and Jerry tried to set a good example and to lay down rules and guidelines, but ultimately they wanted each of their children to become his own person — whoever that person might be.

Jerry worshiped his two boys, and Betty was thrilled to have been able to provide him with the sons that he so clearly adored. However, Betty was secretly scared that something might happen to one of the youngsters because of the impact that such a loss would have on both Jerry and the remaining child. She felt that losing one of his sons would be devastating for Jerry (she was probably right) and that he would most likely compensate by spoiling the other boy. She didn't want either one to happen and, for no real reason, carried that fear with her for a great deal of Mike and Jack's early childhoods. She was completely devoted to her husband and children, and was beginning to find her whole identity through her family role.

She did, however, manage to find some time for socializing and getting together with other political wives. As soon as she was able, Betty put both Mike and Jack into nursery school. She didn't do this because she hated to be around them, she simply did what most mothers did at that time. She found that the children were able to socialize and develop friendships better in that environment than they could at home with nobody their age with whom to play. She also found that the brief respite each day allowed her to develop friendships and to socialize with people such as Mamie Eisenhower, Eisenhower's daughter-in-law Barbara, and Dottie Schultz, the wife of President Eisenhower's aide. Although Betty developed a closer relationship with Barbara since their children were the same age and played together, she learned a great deal from interacting with Mamie Eisenhower. The warm and personal manner she employed when greeting guests and interacting with people was something that Betty would later use herself as the first lady.

Despite the time that Betty was able to carve out for herself, and the help she received from Clara, the fact remained that they lived in a small apartment. No amount of assistance or personal time could compensate for the fact that the Fords needed more space. Shortly after Jack was born, Betty began to campaign aggressively for a house that they could call their own. She would often remind Jerry that "we're wall to wall with tricycles and toys."[3] By this time, Jerry and

Betty were beginning to regret that they hadn't bought a house sooner. They hadn't because they did not really know whether they would be staying in Washington for very long. For one thing, Jerry might have disliked politics and may have decided that a life in public service was not for him. Moreover, they realized that things were much less stable for a first term congressperson than for an incumbent. As time went on, however, it became pretty clear that Jerry wasn't about to go home to Michigan to resume a career in law. He loved being a congressperson and had his sights on one day becoming the Speaker of the House. Having been re-elected three times — by increasing margins each time — it was obvious that the position was his for as long as he wanted it. Jerry Ford's district was one of the safest around and until he decided that he wanted something else, he was going to have a secure place in Congress. Taking everything into consideration, it was pretty clear that Betty, Jerry, Mike, and Jack were going to be in Washington for quite some time. The Fords began to look for a house.

In Alexandria, Virginia there was a tract of land that was being opened up for residential development and the Fords were among the first to purchase a lot in the area. The sidewalks were being poured, and only one other couple, Harriet and Wendell Thorne, had committed to living on Crown View Drive. The lot purchased by the Fords was number 514 Crown View Drive, and the Thornes were to live across the street. With the lot in place, Jerry and Betty began to look over blueprints and to hire a contractor. They settled on a modest, yet comfortable, split-level home with plenty of room for four.

The home was the perfect setting to raise a family during the mid-1950s with plenty of open space for the kids to run around (there were, after all, only two houses on the block), and any number of trees to climb and piles of dirt in which to play. While Betty and Clara had tended to be very particular about Mike's appearance when he was very young, by the time the family got ready to move into the Crown View house they were both much more relaxed. They had learned that children love to play and that they simply will get dirty. Mike was now five, Jack was three, and trying to keep them both clean at all times was simply an exercise in futility. Mike and Jack would roam the neighborhood discovering snakes, getting cookies and snacks from the Thornes, and getting very dirty in the red clay of Virginia — life was good.

Betty still spent a great deal of time ushering around many of Jerry's constituents. She also helped out in his office on occasion since this was often the only way she would get to see him for any extended period of time. Her efforts were greatly appreciated and Jerry even thought about putting her on his payroll until an aide advised him against it. Jerry had brought up the subject because other congressmen were paying their wives, and the new house on Crown Drive was certainly a financial burden. She worked, so why not get paid? His aide insisted that, while putting her on his staff was certainly legal, paying her would be misconstrued by the people back home and would run counter to Jerry's whole philosophy of public service. Jerry agreed and Betty continued to work for free. Betty also spent much of her time decorating the house and working in the garden. She bought new furniture for the house, and attempted to augment the meager amount of landscaping provided by their contractor. Then, Betty and Jerry learned that their family was about to get even larger. Prior to moving into the home, the two had been trying to expand the family — but to no avail. They had assumed that two children would be it, and they made plans accordingly. Betty would later state that, had she known that they would have more children, she would have built a house with more bedrooms and bathrooms. As surprised as they were, Betty and Jerry eagerly anticipated the newest addition to the Ford family.

There had once been a time when Betty had wanted to have another boy to serve as a backup to Jack and Mike. She simply could not shake the fear in the back of her mind that Jerry would be devastated if something were to happen to either Jack or Mike, and that the living child would be spoiled. Over time, however, she had been able to overcome this irrational notion and was now hoping for a girl. She even had a girl's name picked out — she'd actually had the name picked out since the day they were married, just in case. Betty wanted to name the newest Ford addition Sally Meigs Ford. Sally was for a neighbor growing up named Sally Stekee, and Meigs was for her stepfather, Arthur Meigs Godwin. Betty thought that the child could go by Sally, Meigs, or even Meg. When the Fords' third son was born on May 19, 1956, Betty didn't have a name picked out because she had been entirely ready to have Sally Meigs. Betty finally settled on Steven Meigs Ford. She was sulking a bit because she didn't get her girl, but she dearly loved her little boy, Steve.

The summer after Steve was born, Betty decided that she needed a little vacation and took the two older boys to stay in a lakeside cottage at Ottowa Beach. Clara temporarily moved into the Crown View house to look after Steve while the rest of the family was away. Unfortunately for Betty, what was supposed to be a relaxing time with her two older sons turned into something of a surreal nightmare. Jerry and Betty were convinced that the boys would love the beach, but they never got to really experience it. Once Betty and the boys got settled into the cottage, it began to rain, and rain, and then rain some more. The bulk of their time was spent going to the store for candy or sitting around while Betty attempted to come up with games and activities to entertain her two sons of four and six. It was not very relaxing. When Jerry would call to ask how things were going, Betty would tell him that it was "horrible!" Of course, it would stop raining on the weekends when Jerry was out of session and was able to come visit. He would play with the boys, splash in the water, and comment that it was absolutely gorgeous and that he wasn't too sure what Betty was always complaining about. Once he would go back to Washington, it would start to rain again — and clear up when he returned. As if the weeks weren't bad enough, she felt as if he believed she was inventing her own misery. She longed for home and for time with her newest son, Steve. She was feeling a little sorry for herself and just wanted the whole episode to end. She also decided that her next vacation would need to be with just herself and Jerry.

Shortly after the ill-fated "vacation" with the boys, Betty's step-father, Arthur Meigs Godwin, passed away and left her a little bit of money. The frugal side of Jerry and Betty decided that he would have wanted them to pay off their home. They were probably right given Mr. Godwin's generally sensible nature, however, their adventurous, less-cautious side won out and they went on a trip to Europe instead. This time they left all of the children with Clara and went with another couple, Jack and Phoebe Stiles. Jerry could never quite leave work behind, so Betty was glad that she had the Stiles along for some company. The trip turned out to be very enlightening for Betty and probably helped to shape her approach to the office of first lady later in life. Prior to this vacation, Betty had lived a rather sheltered existence and had not been exposed to life outside of the United States. She was both thrilled and shocked by what she saw.

Betty adored Spain and was eager to try everything they had to offer. She fell in love with the flamenco dancers (naturally, given her love for dance), was fascinated by Jai Alai, and even thought that the ornate decorations in the buildings were something to behold. She was even up for going to a bullfight, but that never came to fruition. She would later state that she wasn't necessarily into the idea of the bullfight so much as she was caught up in the moment and would have thought it was the thing to do. Betty also had a splendid time in Italy, but was somewhat disturbed by what she saw in Austria.

Growing up in Grand Rapids, and living a rather sheltered life in the United States, could not prepare Betty for her first hand experience with the ravages of war. The Hungarian uprising of 1956 resulted in a large number of people crossing over into Austria seeking refuge. People would arrive with little more than the clothes on their back, or with what little belongings they were able to carry. The accommodations were less than luxurious, as these people were sleeping on straw and were without even the most rudimentary of plumbing systems. It was cold and the refugees, many of them babies and young children, lacked adequate clothing to keep them warm against the elements. Betty has remarked that despite the language barrier and inability to speak with the people,

New Job, New Family

"you could tell by the strain on their faces what they'd been through."[4] In short, Betty felt a combination of helplessness and guilt. She realized that there was not much that she could do to help, and that anything she could do would really amount to very little in the grand scheme of things. She also felt guilty because she was here on a vacation — that she could afford the luxury of travel and that life was generally very good for her and her family. This, she realized, was something that she had taken for granted. This revelation would help to shape many of her actions later in life — especially as first lady.

The Vienna experience wasn't the only negative aspect of the Fords' European vacation,

Betty wasn't nearly as thrilled with the restaurants and food as the rest of the experience. While Jerry and their companions had no trouble with the cuisine, Betty was sick much of the time and the mere thought of food made her nauseous at times. There was a reason. Prior to their departure for Europe, Betty had gone to her physician, Dr. Chin, for a post-natal examination. She didn't think that she was experiencing any problems but wanted to make sure that everything was okay since she would be overseas for several weeks. After the doctor had given her the routine examination, he informed her that he thought she was pregnant. Betty didn't believe the doctor. After all, Steve was only six months old and there had been greater space between all of her children. Besides, she had become convinced that three children was enough and she and Jerry had taken precautions to avoid another pregnancy. Dr. Chin had to have been mistaken. All through Europe, Betty had problems with nausea and with the foreign food. She attributed the problems to "tourista." As her "tourista" became more frequent, yet inconsistent, she started to wonder whether the Dr. had been correct in his assessment. By the time they were about to head home, Betty was pretty sure the doctor was right — she was pregnant again.

The first thing Betty did upon returning home was to schedule another appointment with Dr. Chin. She humbly admitted that he was right, that she was pregnant, and that she was ready. She didn't say it at the time, but she was most certainly getting geared up for another long pregnancy since all three of her boys had gone past term. She was also getting prepared for another son. Having been disappointed before, she wasn't about to set herself up for a letdown again. Besides, Grandma Ford had four sons so it seemed almost destiny that Betty would too. At least she thought it was her destiny to follow in the elder Mrs. Ford's footsteps in this regard.

Betty finally had her little girl, Susan Elizabeth, on July 6, 1957. Betty distinctly remembers the day and time for a couple of very strange reasons that go beyond the normal motherly memory of childbirth. First, she remembers missing the family's traditional Fourth of July picnic with neighborhood friends because she felt that she was too pregnant to attend. Not that Betty was any danger of losing the child, she didn't want to attend because she thought that her condition made her look like a tugboat. While everyone would have certainly understood her appearance and probably would have fawned over her for it, Betty held her ground and sent Jerry and the two older boys off without her. This was a small foreshadowing of the second reason Betty distinctly remembers the day and time of Susan's birth — it was Mickey Mantle day at the ballpark. The day began with Betty waking up sweaty and swollen from a very hot, humid, summer day in Virginia that coincided with yet another long pregnancy. She started to cry and just wanted her baby to be born and for the discomfort to end. According to her, she actually cried herself into labor. Fortunately, Jerry was home because it was Mickey Mantle day. He normally worked on Saturdays but this day was special because he was going to take Mike and Jack to watch the Yankees play the Washington team. Above all, they were going to see Yankee great, Mickey Mantle, who was the boyhood idol of both Mike and Jack (from the sounds of things, Jerry was also a big fan). When Betty went into labor, Jerry was there to rush her to the hospital. According to Betty, he drove like the wind to get her admitted — not for her sake, but because he didn't want to miss the 1:00 game. Even the doctor seems to have been caught up in the excitement of Mickey Mantle day because, when informed that Jerry wouldn't be at the hospital because of the game, he asked where they were sitting so he could watch for them on television. Even Dr. Chin was watching the game. Betty was experiencing labor pains and the doctor, Jerry, and the kids were all enjoying a nice afternoon baseball game. Betty couldn't help but feel as if she and her new baby were somehow being discounted. She has remarked, with a bit of sarcasm, "Susan was very cooperative. She was born in the seventh inning stretch, so we didn't disturb anybody."[5] With the birth of Susan, the Ford family was complete.

IMPORTANT HIGHLIGHTS

By the time the children were born, Betty's new identity had been partly shaped. The political partnership was in full swing and Betty was making the rounds at all of the right functions and was entertaining Jerry's constituents when called upon. She was Mrs. Jerry Ford and she was helping him in his meteoric rise on Capitol Hill! With the birth of their four children, the creation of Betty's mid-life identity would be almost complete. Mrs. Ford has often remarked that her family comes first. In many cases, this has meant that she came second, or even third. This willingness to give of herself has had both positive and negative consequences. Her open, caring nature is one of her most endearing attributes and is very much a part of the Betty Ford that people know and will always remember. On the downside, self-sacrifice has not always been healthy for Betty Ford.

Chapter 5

BETTY'S IDENTITY

When Betty and Jerry built their house on Crown View, they had assumed that there would only be two Ford children living in the home. With four bedrooms, this meant that each child could have his own room and there would still be a guestroom. When Steven was born, Betty still figured that her cherished guestroom would be intact since two of the boys could share a room. She was still thinking of ways to maintain guest space when she assumed that Susan would also be male. Jerry and Betty would share one room, there would be two boys to a room, and there would be a fourth room left for guests. Apparently Jerry felt that guest space was important too since once Susan was born he jokingly remarked, "There goes the guestroom."[1] He was kidding, but the remark held a certain amount of truth to it. The family had expanded but the infrastructure remained fairly stagnant — both in terms of house space and income.

Congresspeople today make considerably more than they did in the 1950s and Jerry's income, while sufficient to live comfortably, was being stretched to its limits. They began to worry about saving enough money for college and about having enough money to raise four children and still maintain the comfortable lifestyle to which they had become accustomed. It had already been determined that Betty couldn't receive payment for her work assisting Jerry in the office and attending to visiting constituents, so they began to discuss their options. They would occasionally talk about how there was still time for Jerry to return to Grand Rapids and resume his career in law. He was in his forties, and there was still time to become established in the legal community and make a good amount of money. For the first time since they had come to Washington, the Fords began to think about leaving public life. At least Betty began to think about it — it seems as though Jerry was merely tossing around the idea and speculating after a particularly rough day at work. According to Ford biographer, Jerald F. terHorst, "these were private inner thoughts that he shared only with Betty at home after a hard day on the Hill. He had no firm plan to retire or change jobs; it was just an idea nestled deep in his mind that, from time to time, he brought forward for polishing and then returned to its niche."[2] Jerry Ford was the consummate politician and he was very much a political animal who loved what he did for a living. Despite any imagined financial strains, the Fords were going to remain in Washington for quite some time, and Gerald Ford was going to remain in Congress.

To compensate for the fact that they weren't going to be extremely wealthy, Betty did her best to make the most of what they had. This is not to suggest that they were wanting for anything — it merely points to the fact that Betty became the household manager. She was in charge of balancing the family checkbook and for keeping track of the finances. She also made the most of what they already owned. In her case, she was able to forego buying new clothes for a long time because she had been able to amass a substantial wardrobe while working at Herpolscheimer's. She was fortunate to have been able to acquire a lot of clothes that didn't go out of fashion, and she made use of them for as long as she could. Betty probably would have been fairly frugal anyway given the way that the Bloomers rallied together during the depression — she was raised to not be too frivolous and to make the most of what was on hand. The Fords weren't wanting, but they weren't wasteful either. It also points to the fact that Betty had to do many things that wealthy families hired people to do. The Fords were a typical middle-class family whose children went to public school, and the mother was an all-around jack-of-all-trades. To suggest that stay at home mothers do not work would be a great misconception. With four children and a husband whose work keeps him away from home for great periods of time, the workload is increased substantially. Betty Ford was extremely busy! In addition to being the family bookkeeper, Betty was a member of the local PTA, was involved with other congressional wives in various civic affairs, and was even the program chairperson for the Alexandria Cancer Fund Drive. As a mother and wife, Betty felt she was expected to do just about everything. While others may not have expected her to be superwoman, Betty threw herself into her various roles as though she was.

Betty cooked. Jerry has written that, despite his frequent absences, he was a committed family man. From the time he first stepped into his role as the congressman from Grand Rapids, he was on the road almost constantly and he found that maintaining any semblance of a regular presence at home was next to impossible. To compensate, he would always carve Sunday out of his schedule to be at home with Betty and the children. The one constant in all of their lives was the Sunday reunion. The family would all go to church and then return home for a big brunch of bacon, sausage, eggs, waffles, and fruit. After visiting during the day, they would all sit down together for a roast beef dinner. Jerry and the children always looked forward to the Sunday meals and even came to expect them. Of course, this meant that Betty got to cook. The one day that Jerry was home to relax and spend time with the family was the one day that Betty had to cook the most.

Betty chauffeured. Clara was a great help to the Fords, but Betty's primary responsibility was to raise the children. This often included taking them to the doctor and to school. She also took the children to any extracurricular activities and social gatherings in which they might be engaged. She didn't go so far as to drive the children on dates in their later years, but she did do her fair share of driving and chauffeuring. From Sunday school and scouts, to football practice and doctor's appointments, Betty was there for all of them. With four children, there is always something going on, and someone has to get them there. In the case of the Ford family, that someone was Betty.

Betty played zookeeper. Most children like to have pets and to raise various types of animals, and the Ford children were no exception. They had gerbils, birds, fish, rabbits, chickens, turtles, cats, and even praying mantises. Unfortunately, when children raise pets, the bulk of the responsibility often falls on the parents. This is especially true as the novelty of a new pet wears off. There are some creatures, however, that even a parent doesn't want to deal with. For the Fords, the one animal that Betty didn't want to take care of was the family alligator. Someone had sent them the creature when it was still young and small. As with all living creatures, however, the alligator grew. Eventually Jack and Mike had to build a box for the alligator outdoors — this was one pet that the boys did take care of. Betty thought that the alligator was a vile pet and tended to grimace every time the boys went out to handle the thing. It grew to be about four feet long and would turn on the boys every chance it got. They had to catch live food for the alligator and needed to wear boxing gloves when they fed the thing so they wouldn't get bit themselves. They had to tie a rope around its neck in order to take it out of the box, and it went after them the moment it got free of the rope. Finally, Betty had seen enough. She decided that the alligator needed to stay outside at all times — even though she knew that the weather was about to get cold. If it survived, it survived. It didn't. After one particular frost-filled evening, Jack came into the house to tell his mother that the alligator wasn't moving. Betty asked him if he thought that, perhaps, the creature had gotten so cold that it died of pneumonia. Jack thought that this explanation made sense, but added, "I should have protected him."[3] Betty felt horrible and saddened that Jack would bear such guilt over the loss of the alligator. She was, however glad to be rid of the beast.

Betty was a den mother and Sunday school teacher. With three boys, it was inevitable that cub scouts would become a part of the Ford family. As soon as the children were old enough, Mike, Jack, and Steve all became scouts. Betty did her part too, by being the den mother for a cub scout pack of energetic young boys. As den mother, she had to come up with activities to occupy their time once a week when they met. When it was nice, they could go outside and play games. When the weather was less cooperative, they had to opt for indoor activities — generally arts and crafts. Everyone had a great time — including Betty who earned high marks from the children because of her ability to turn cartwheels. Still, while there is no question that all of those concerned had a wonderful time, Betty still refers to her den mother experience as putting in "three years' hard time."[4] She also put in some hard time as a Sunday school teacher at the Emmanuel-on-the-Hill Episcopal Church of Alexandria from 1961-1964. She didn't feel that it was her strong suit, but she did feel that she had a certain obligation. It wouldn't be fair for her to shove her four children off on somebody else when she hadn't done her part too. With that in mind, Betty became a Sunday school teacher in addition to being a chef, zookeeper, den mother and chauffeur (among other things).

One incident illustrates Betty's occasional struggle with being a Sunday school teacher yet also serves as an appropriate segue into any discussion of her approach to raising children. She had the misfortune of having the minister's son as one of the students in her class. He was, without doubt, the worst student that she had to face. He was mean, unruly, and disrespectful. Since his father was the minister, he approached everything as if he owned the place and he simply didn't need to mind anybody. On one particular occasion he decided that instead of heeding Betty's directions, he should just hit her. He hit her squarely in the face. She told him if that made him feel good, he should do it again. He did. Unfazed, Betty continued to insist that he follow directions like the rest of the children. When he raised his hand for a third time, Betty lost it and smacked him on the butt. To her, this was *his* victory because she lost her temper and lowered herself to his level. She didn't believe in spanking, and didn't rely on the practice in raising her own children. Instead, she would reason with the children and explain, that with six people living in the house, they would simply have to learn to get along and coexist peacefully. When that didn't work, she would have the offending child leave the room and think about what they might to do handle the situation better. Spanking was not part of the Ford household (except for a very rare whack on the bottom that she has equated with the benign practice of smacking a puppy on the nose with newspaper — it is the sound and the motion more than the force). Understanding Betty's approach to discipline is important to understand because, in addition to all of her other roles, Betty was the family peacemaker and disciplinarian.

Since Jerry was gone most of the time, the day to day raising and disciplining of the children fell to Betty. In other words, she got to play the same role as that of her mother, Hortense, who was forced into raising the children alone when William Bloomer was away on business. According to daughter Susan, "she was, I wouldn't say a single mother, but she did a lot of it alone. We had a wonderful housekeeper, but four kids is four kids." It was Betty who laid out the ground rules for the family to follow and who molded the childrens' character and helped to shape them into the people they would become. It was Betty who set curfews and who meted out punishment when the children got out of line. She did this, not only because she was the only parent there to do so, but because she felt it was part of her job as Jerry's wife to eliminate any external stress from *his* life. She knew he worked hard and that she and the children got to see very little of him. When he was home, she wanted him to be able to relax and to spend some quality time with the family — not spend time dealing with domestic squabbles and reprimanding the children. In her words, "I took care of those things so we could all enjoy each others company when he was at home."[5] In other words, she carried all of the stress of marriage and parenthood so that Jerry could enjoy the benefits. She did this despite the fact that he could never even manage to be around for their anniversary because it fell during the heart of campaign season. This is not to suggest that Gerald Ford was a selfish man, it merely points out that he was a very busy man who happened to have a very understanding, loving, caring woman by his side — although he may have taken her for granted from time to time.

Betty was a political sidekick and social companion. Aside from helping in Jerry's office, and ushering around visiting constituents, Betty was also expected to attend various social functions, either with Jerry or on his behalf. As an emerging figure in national politics, Jerry was invited to a large number of social/political events and Betty was by his side for almost all of them. While with him, however, she seldom exhibited much of her own personality or her own opinion on any matters of importance. While she certainly felt very strongly about certain issues, she believed that her opinions belonged at home and that Jerry was the politician. Taking a more conservative, traditional approach to her role in the partnership, Betty preferred to be seen, not heard (in public), and to shelter her family from the limelight. This approach was commented on early in Gerald Ford's congressional career by one writer who stated, "Mrs. Ford believes that wives of congressmen look better on a speaking platform when they're saying nothing. She leaves the politics to her husband."[6] While politics is an inherent function of being a congressperson, Jerry took his politics to ever increasing levels and his constant striving for political success kept him away from home for longer periods of time. This placed an added burden on Betty to maintain the image of the perfect mother and political wife.

As Betty increasingly threw herself into her role as wife and mother, Jerry's stock in the Republican Party rose dramatically. He was easily being reelected each time he ran, and was becoming quite a force within the power structure of the House of Representatives. He was so well respected that the American Political Science Association bestowed upon him an honor for distinguished service, and dubbed him a "Congressman's Congressman." This was only the beginning. In 1963, Jerry was the focal point for an uprising within the ranks of the Republican party as several of the younger members — the "Young Turks" — moved to wrest power from some of the senior, more established, members of the House. Their first target was Representative Charles Hoeven of Iowa who happened to be the close friend of House Minority Leader, Charles Halleck. Lacking the power to strike out at Halleck directly, this small group of party members sought to send him a message by ousting Hoeven instead. In a close vote, Gerald Ford became the chairman of the House Republican Conference — a very powerful position. The primary reason that Ford was elected was that he was well liked and respected by everyone in the party. He wasn't the architect of the Young Turk's coup, but he was a beneficiary. He was well liked and well respected by those around him and he was the obvious choice for those wanting to make a change — he was younger and more open minded than many of the more established members, yet he wasn't so radical that his appointment would lead to any wholesale changes. Regardless of the reasons, Gerald Ford was on the move and he secretly had his sights set on the top party leadership spot and hopefully, one day, the Speaker of the House.

As Jerry was making his mark within the party and within national politics, he was really finding himself and establishing his identity. At the same time, Betty was in the process of losing hers. On the outside, Betty appeared to be holding herself and the family together quite well. On the inside, Betty was struggling with a loss of self. This once strongly independent woman who had been both aspiring dancer and professional woman, was now known as Mrs. Ford or the mother of Mike, Jack, Steve, and Susan. She had, in a sense, given up two careers that had helped to form her identity. These were replaced by an identity that was intertwined with, and even dependent upon, the identity of others. While she loved being a wife and mother, she was forgetting that Betty mattered too.

Chapter 6

1964-1973

1964 started out just as any other year, with the children actively engaged in their own activities, with Betty's support, and Jerry actively engaged in his activities, again with Betty's support. Among Jerry's activities was the Republican National Convention. As an established, yet still rising, star within the party, Jerry played a key role in the party's grandest occasion. The 1964 convention, the Goldwater-Miller convention, was no exception and Jerry was away from home almost around the clock to make sure that the event ran smoothly. As consolation, Jerry had agreed to take some much deserved vacation time — deserved for him and Betty. The plan was for the entire family to spend a couple of weeks at a beach in Delaware and to simply unwind, relax, and be a family. They had rented a cottage at Bethany Beach, and were getting set to go, when trouble struck.

Only two days before they were all scheduled to leave for their much anticipated vacation, Betty was awakened during the night by a severe pain in her neck. Her injury occurred as the result of something as normal as opening and closing a door — in this case, it was simply opening a kitchen window. One afternoon, Betty Ford raised a kitchen window and, without knowing it, would, to a certain extent, change her life. She was somehow in an awkward position and pinched a nerve in her neck. While she didn't feel anything at the time, she had caused damage. She awoke later that night with a terrible pain in her neck that shot all of the way down her arm. The pain was so intense that she couldn't get back to sleep. Needless to say, she was scared, but true to form, went downstairs to suffer in silence so as to not disturb Jerry or the children. She always put her own needs behind those of her family. Jerry found her downstairs the next morning, lying on the couch in obvious discomfort. He took her to the emergency room where they told her that it was a pinched nerve — no big deal — and that she just needed to go home and rest. The doctors placed her in a soft collar, gave her a prescription for Darvon, and sent her home. Rest didn't seem to make any difference, so Jerry and Betty went to the National Orthopedic Hospital where Betty was placed in traction and given additional medication for the pain.

As always, Betty thought of herself last and insisted that, since she was laid up in the hospital, the family should go on the vacation to Delaware without her. Despite the fact that she was desperately in need of some vacation time, she didn't want the rest of the family to suffer with her. Jerry and the children left, as planned, and Betty remained behind, strapped to a traction device. After a week, Jerry returned to see how she was doing and found that she was still in traction and that the pain was just a severe as when she was first admitted. Finally Betty was sent home, but was requiring a larger amount of pain medication and still needed to rest. She was home, but still bed-ridden and strapped to a traction device that Jerry had built for her to use at home. She was miserable!

Not only did the injury leave Betty unable to stand straight, it forced her to hold her arm at an awkward angle. In her words, "I could have played the *Hunchback of Notre Dame.*"[1] Unfortunately, the pain did not want to go away. She continued therapy and sought the advice of many doctors over a five year period. Eventually, she was diagnosed with a mild form of osteoarthritis, a condition that can impact women as they grow older (it can affect men too, but is more common in women). The combination of the pinched nerve, which never went away, and the development of arthritis, left Betty with physical pain that has been with her to this day. As a "single mother" of four, the pain was something that Betty willed herself to endure. Jerry had his job, and she had hers. She slowly worked herself up to where she could drive a car, shop, and do most of the things that she had been able to do prior to the injury. She managed to do what she always had — keep up appearances and sacrifice herself for others. Only those closest to her know that the everyday activities of life were more painful for Betty than they are for the rest of us. She simply went about her daily routine without complaining. After all, in her words, "I had a long way to go, four strapping children only half raised, a great responsibility."[2]

Things got worse. If Betty felt that she had to shoulder the responsibility of raising the family while Jerry was away during the early parts of their life together, he was about to make things worse. The Young Turks had decided to set their sights on Charlie Halleck. Instead of simply sending him a message as they had with the ousting of Charles Hoeven, the group wanted Halleck out. The Republican Party had suffered some pretty big losses and they wanted to improve their image and portray themselves as being more progressive and fair-minded.

For this, some felt they needed Jerry Ford at the top. Four of the leading Young Turks, Melvin Laird, Charles Goodell, Robert Griffin, and Donald Rumsfeld approached Jerry about his willingness to challenge Halleck for the position of House Minority Leader. Jerry said he would have to discuss it with his family.

Jerry went to Betty and the children with the Young Turk's proposal and told them how becoming the House Minority Leader might help him to someday live out his dream of ascending to the position of Speaker of the House. He also told them that the flip side was that the new post would require even more traveling and that he wouldn't be able to spend as much time with the family. After some deliberations, twelve year old Jack said, "Go for it Dad."[3] That seemed to settle the issue and Jerry told the Young Turks that he would be willing to try and unseat Halleck.

After a close election, Jerry won — by seven votes.

If Jerry was something of an absent father before, the time away from home only increased when Jerry Ford became the Minority Leader in the House of Representatives in January of 1965. While Betty was certainly proud of her husband, she was inwardly sad at the same time. She once commented, "the congress got a new Minority Leader, and I lost a husband." For a time, Jerry was away from home as much as 258 days out of the year. Betty was forced to assume the role her mother had played during Betty's youth — primary care giver. Being alone to serve as a den mother, Sunday-school teacher, chauffeur, and other assorted duties that went along with raising four children, left Betty with even less time for herself than she had before. Even Jerry's needs increased. There were occasions when he would fly back to Washington and head straight to his office without going home to see Betty and the children. He would call Betty to ask her to pack him a suitcase with clean clothes and other items he needed. His driver would swing by the house, drop off his dirty clothes, pick up the clean ones, and be off. Jerry would then fly away again without even a simple hug. Betty's concern was that *he* was driving *himself* too hard. She constantly prayed for his health and was really worried that the heavy schedule was harmful. She didn't really consider the toll that it was taking on her.

Betty was still living in constant pain from the nerve injury and arthritis and was still being stretched as the lone parent and political sidekick. She saw Jerry pushing himself to further the party and decided to shake things up on her own. She saw that Democratic wives were generally more visible in the community and were more effective at bolstering support for their husbands. If Jerry was going to help the cause, so was she, and so were the other Republican wives. Betty took it upon herself to organize charity fashion shows and other events designed to raise money for causes such as multiple sclerosis and heart disease. Betty also increased her role as mother by getting involved in the PTA. In short, Betty was behaving as if she were superhuman. The lack of spousal support and the inconvenience of pain were not going to slow *her* down.

The loss of identity was continuing. Unfortunately, Betty was beginning to feel neglected and taken for granted. Sometimes, she would make jokes about her plight by saying things to Jerry like, "what are you doing here?" when she would see him lying in bed next to her. The jokes were really masking the fact that she needed him and was feeling somewhat resentful of his being gone so much while she was left alone to raise the children. Moreover, she was resentful that the Republican Party got to see much more of her husband than she did and that, somehow, he might care for them more than her. These inner feelings were never shared, but were kept tightly bottled up inside — what Jerry saw was the same supportive, happy, loving wife that he had always seen.

This would change.

Finally, in 1970, the pain, the struggle to remain active as a political wife while having to raise the family by herself, and the lack of personal attention were too much for Betty to handle.

She experienced a nervous breakdown from the strain. All of the emotions and pain she had been keeping inside for years came gushing out in one tremendous emotional outburst. Susan, saw her mother sobbing uncontrollably and, sensing that something was wrong, called their housekeeper Clara Powell. Clara came over to try and calm Betty down and called Jerry home from Sequoia telling him that he needed to be there.

What Jerry found was a woman who had allowed herself to be used up by everyone around her. She was superwoman on the outside but was still human on the inside and still had human needs. Jerry gladly went along with the family doctor's recommendation that Betty see a psychiatrist. In fact, Jerry would have done anything for Betty and he even went to see the psychiatrist himself — despite any potential political risk that such a visit might hold.

Sessions with the psychiatrist made it clear to Betty that she longed for attention. She was hurt by the fact that she did everything for others but they never seemed to reciprocate. She wanted to leave so that the family would wonder where she was and would worry that nobody was around to do all of the things that she did. She wanted them to understand how important she was and that she was taken for granted. In her words, "I wanted them to say, 'well, my gosh, Mother is gone, what are we going to do?'"[4]

Betty saw the psychiatrist twice a week for a couple of years and used him as a sounding board for the things she could never say to Jerry and the kids. While she felt like she had to be strong for them, it was okay to tell the psychiatrist that she was in pain, or that she had fears about the pervasiveness of drugs in the schools, or that she was having a hard time coping with the stress of being both full-time mother and full-time politician's wife. She could also discuss, with a sympathetic ear, the fact that she had lost her own sense of identity and had lost her own sense of self-worth. Through being "mother" — even Jerry called her "mother" — Betty had disappeared. Through these discussions, she began to find herself and began to realize that she had to stop keeping things bottled up inside. According to Betty, "I don't believe in spilling your guts all over the place, but I no longer believe in suffering in silence over something that's really bothering you. I think you have to get it out and on the table and discuss it, no matter what it is."[5] She also learned that it was okay to ask for help and support.

With support from the psychiatrist, Jerry, and her children, Betty slowly began to realize that she didn't have to be superhuman and that she couldn't do everything. Moreover, they made it clear to her that she didn't have to, and that it was important for her to take time for herself and to do things that were important to her. Once she admitted this to herself, a tremendous weight fell from her shoulders and she began to be more assertive about her own needs. One thing that was important to her was for the family to have more time together and for her to get her husband back from the hold of Congress.

Early in 1973 the rumors surrounding the Watergate scandal were running around Washington and things did not look good for the Republican Party. While Jerry had felt the 1972 elections offered some hope that he someday live out his dream of becoming Speaker, the political environment in 1973 led Jerry to reluctantly accept the fact that he would probably never hold the coveted position. This realization, coupled with Betty's recent health problems and desire to spend more time with him, had Jerry seriously contemplating retirement for the first time. He figured that if he ran once more and then left office at the end of Nixon's term (which would be January of 1977), he would be sixty-three and could still practice law or do something to generate some serious income for a few years. He even contemplated spending his last term in a lesser position by passing a great deal of the responsibility onto a younger person whom he could groom to replace him. When he presented these thoughts to Betty, she was elated. After some discussion, Betty and Jerry agreed that he would retire at the end of Richard Nixon's second term in office. They had no reason to believe that anything would change these plans.

Even before Watergate became a household word, Spiro Theodore Agnew, the 39th Vice-President of the United States, had come under investigation by the U.S. attorney in Baltimore for allegedly receiving payoffs from engineers seeking contracts when Agnew was Baltimore county executive and governor of

Maryland. From the time these allegations came out in the early part of 1972, Agnew asserted his innocence, but he then suddenly resigned on Oct. 10, 1973 after pleading no contest to a single charge of income tax evasion. The Fords had been planning on retiring and leaving public life. They had done their part in serving this country and believed it was time for them to focus on themselves and their family. Jerry was still the House Minority Leader, but was very happy dreaming about life after politics. Betty and Jerry were even to the point of contemplating where they would retire, when the resignation of Spiro Agnew as Vice President of the United States changed their plans. In Betty's words, "Spiro Agnew upset our applecart."[6]

The same day as the resignation, Mel Laird called Jerry at home to ask, "Jerry, if you were asked, would you accept the Vice Presidential nomination?"[7] Laird, one of the Young Turks who had helped to elevate Ford to the position of minority leader, was now a member of Nixon's cabinet. Knowing that the call would not come without some urging from Nixon himself, Jerry replied that he would have to think about it and he would call Laird back. Jerry and Betty spent the next several hours discussing the pros and cons of accepting the nomination. Obvious negatives were that the family would be placed under the media spotlight and some of the privacy they had worked so hard to maintain would disappear and that the office of the vice president doesn't have much to do. Jerry didn't really relish the thought of slowing down and having less of an impact. Another negative was the uncertainty over the future — would Jerry be expected to run in 1976 after they had their sights set on retirement? On the plus side, the position would be something of a crowning achievement and a cap on a splendid career. It wasn't the Speaker position, but it would be some recognition for all of Jerry's years of hard work for both the Republican Party and the country. Despite the negatives, they agreed that he should accept the offer if there were, in fact, an official nomination. They still weren't convinced that Jerry would get the call.

With Agnew gone, there was bound to be speculation that Gerald Ford would be named as successor to the vice presidency, but neither Betty nor Jerry really thought it would happen (after all, they reasoned, he was too important for the party in Congress). Betty was so certain that Gerald would not be named (she felt it would be John Connally) that she made a five dollar bet with her daughter, Susan — Betty lost. Nixon submitted Gerald Ford's name to Congress on October 13, 1973. After a very short set of confirmation hearings (Jerry's long ties to Congress and knowledge that he would not face much opposition was a major reason why he received the nomination over bigger names such as Connally, Rockefeller, and Reagan), Jerry was confirmed by the Senate on November 27 and by the House on December 6 — neither vote was even close. Gerald Ford was sworn in as the 40th Vice President of the United States, and the first to assume the position under provisions set forth by the 25th Amendment to the Constitution, on the evening of December 6, 1973. As always, Betty was by his side — something that did not go unnoticed by Jerry. As he looked out over Congress, he stood at the podium and paused to state to the masses, but more for the benefit of his family, "standing by my side, as she always has, there are no words to tell you (Congress) ....my dear wife, and mother of our four children, how much their being here means to me."[8]

Betty was excited for her husband but was inwardly saddened that their retirement plans might be put on hold. She was also somewhat scared about the uncertainty that lay ahead and the amount of press that she would be expected to address. While Betty was disappointed and scared, she put on her game face and pushed forward. According to Leesa Tobin, an archivist for the Ford library, Betty "responded as a true politician's wife."[9] Betty reportedly stated, "well, if they just wind me up and point me in the right direction, I'll be there."[10]

PART 2: THE EXECUTIVE BRANCH

Chapter 7

ONE STEP-AWAY

Despite the new position, which placed Jerry one step away from being the most powerful person on the planet, the Fords were determined to keep things as normal as possible for their family. There had been the possibility of the family moving into the Admiralty House, a property purchased by the government for use by the Vice President, but it wasn't yet functional. They weren't too disappointed; the house on Crown View Drive was where they had made a home, and it was where they were going to stay. The only real downside to staying on Crown View Drive was that the home was originally designed with two adults and two children in mind, and it was a fairly tight space for just the family. When the added presence of secret service agents and the onslaught of reporters was thrown into the mix, it was extremely cramped.

Right after Jerry was sworn in, the secret service had swarmed over their home like insects. Since the house was beyond full, the agents had to resort to using the garage as a command center and place of residence. They simply put the bicycles and assorted toys out into the yard. The car lost its home and was a permanent fixture in the driveway. Despite moving all of the items out of their way, the fact remained that it was still a garage. Jerry felt somewhat sorry for them and shelled out $10,000 of his own money so that the garage could be converted into a guesthouse. The agents, once comfortably situated, continued in their job of protecting the Vice President. This job included installing sentry boxes to keep watch, and placing high security locks on all of the doors to the home. The locks and constant security presence was somewhat disturbing for Betty who was generally accustomed to a more simple existence. She had long ago lost the keys to their house — there was no need to lock the doors in their neighborhood — and the thought of someone constantly rising to open doors every time she entered into a room was a bit overwhelming. She eventually adjusted, but was never fully at ease with the constant attention and rigid security measures — until there was a threat on Susan.

At first, Jerry was the only member of the family with full-time protection. All of the rest of them were only protected when they were at home. This changed one Friday afternoon shortly after Jerry was sworn in. The secret service called Betty to inform her that she should not let Susan go out that weekend and that she was to remain inside the house. Apparently Susan's name had been on a list of three people being targeted by a group known as the Symbionese Liberation Army (SLA). Of the people on the list, one had been shot and killed, one other, Patty Hearst, had been kidnapped. The only person left was Susan, the daughter of the new Vice President — despite their desire to remain normal, it wasn't going to happen.

Life with a suburban family led to some adjustment on the part of the agents too. Especially a family with four children — two of them still living at home and going to high school. In addition to the stress of the SLA affair, there was the constant pressure from the children to allow them to lead normal lives and spend time with their friends. In the case of Susan, this meant a lot of parties being held in the Ford home. Another adjustment had to be made for seventeen year old Steve. One particularly tense moment came on a January morning when Steve's friend, Bobby Hanback, came over to start their day. The plan was for Bobby and Steve to spend the day quail hunting in the woods close by. Unfortunately for Bobby, he didn't think anything about approaching the home with a shotgun slinging over his shoulder — he was instantly surrounded by tense secret service agents. After Steve finally convinced them that everything was okay, and that Bobby wasn't a threat to anyone, things returned to normal and the agents went back to their positions. Eventually, the agents grew accustomed to the various long-haired teens in jeans that frequented the home and they were able to tell who belonged and who did not.

As a parent, there were some "perks" to having the agents around the house. Jerry has commented that the daily arrival and departure logs were a great asset to a parent trying to raise an attractive teenage daughter. Susan led a fairly active social life but was still a student whose parents wanted her to be home by eleven on school nights. Since Jerry and Betty were usually tired and in bed by that time, they couldn't really monitor when she got in. Sometimes, for fun, Jerry would ask Susan what time she got home. When she would reply, "early," Jerry could have some fun. Before the omnipresent security detail, there was no way of knowing. Now there were the logs. Jerry could now say, "well I think I'll check on that" — much to Susan's chagrin and Jerry's delight.[1]

The "normal" routine was also changed by the number of social engagements that Betty and Jerry were required to attend. Jerry has indicated that, as Minority Leader, he might receive between forty and fifty social invitations a week, but as the Vice President the number of invitations escalated to around five hundred per week. The Fords had definitely moved up the social ladder.

While Betty was determined to keep things as normal as possible for the children, she seemed to enjoy being the second lady (wife of the vice president). Her initial discomfort with the security and overly courteous manner of the agents was overridden by the fact that she was able to get some much-needed help. She didn't have to make beds, or do some of the house work that she had always done. She also had someone to do the cooking, although the tempting food that the naval stewards produced made it hard for her to stick to the diet she had been on for the past year. During her bought with depression she had ballooned to around 140 pounds and had managed to drop down to the 110 that made her feel comfortable. They even hired a personal assistant for Betty to keep up with the correspondence she was receiving and to help her keep track of the active social calendar. Nancy Howe, her assistant, was the wife of an army officer and had been a part of the White House Historical Commission. Nancy knew her way around Washington and was basically Betty's "right arm" since she scheduled speaking engagements, made travel plans and arrangements, and even helped to answer letters. Between the secret service agents, the naval stewards, and Nancy Howe, Betty was given the opportunity to finally relax and enjoy being herself for the first time in a great while.

She was able to be herself, but not quite in the private manner she was hoping. With the new position came a new set of challenges and obligations. She was no longer a House of Representatives wife, but a Senate wife — being married to the vice president carries with it the presidency of the Red Cross Senate Wives. She was also expected to adjust to life as a member of the executive branch of government that is quite different than being a member of the House. Betty also got involved with other causes. She would spend time at Goodwill Industries — an employer of workers with physical challenges — in order to simply talk with the people and share something of herself with them. She became a mainstay with the National Endowment for the Arts by advancing special programs that served underprivileged and disabled children. She even started the "art train" which was an attempt to bring artists and great art to parts of the country that had never had much exposure to them. The elevation to second lady seemed to allow her to become active in a number of areas that mattered to her. The ability to pick and choose projects was something different for Betty.

The biggest difference in the transition from congressman's wife to second lady, however, was the media attention.

Even before Jerry became vice president, the media was becoming something of a presence on Crown View Drive. The press had a feeling that Jerry might get the nomination and certain reporters wanted to make sure they got the story before anyone else. David Kennerly of *Time* magazine was one such reporter. He was actually hedging his bet by photographing all of the potential nominees. When he called to see if he could take Jerry's picture, he was told to save his film because, in Jerry's words, "It's not going to be me."[2] Kennerly ignored Jerry and set up the photo shoot so that he would have a cover photo waiting. This attention was nothing! Once the nomination was official, the media swarmed. Since the secret service wouldn't allow them onto the Fords' property, most of the reporters and camera crew stationed themselves across the street at the home of Pete and Louise Abbruzzese. Pete and Louis were actually quite hospitable and allowed them to use the garage to stay dry and even served them an occasional martini. All of the media camped out waiting to see if they could get a story must have been quite a sight. Some members of the media were luckier than others were.

Dick Cavett was a very big name in television at the time, and he traveled to Virginia to capture the Fords at home. In order for this to take place, however, the crew had to move most of the furniture outside. It was a mild day so most people thought that no harm could come of the move. Betty looked out the window and saw that the crew had placed her furniture under a tree that was full of birds — she wasn't worried about rain anymore. Betty basically panicked and called Nancy on the phone to come down and save the furniture by saying, "get down there as fast as you can and tell them to get that stuff covered up so the birds don't decorate it."[3] This was only the beginning of the wonderful time that the Fords spent with Dick Cavett. The crew crammed several pieces of large equipment into the small home while Jerry, Betty, Susan, Steve, and Dick Cavett were all shoved into a small corner. The underfurnished corner was supposed to convey a feeling of intimacy, but it really just felt cramped. Dick Cavett was sitting in a chair with Steve standing by his side answering such inane questions as, "do you think I could learn to ski?" Steve was clearly unimpressed and the whole family felt awkward. The interview lasted several hours and it was unpleasant for everyone. Later Betty would say, "I was never so glad to see a bunch of people get out in my life."[4]

Betty's most famous interview as second lady took place with a number of guidelines put into place. Betty, being somewhat new to the interview game, was apprehensive and wanted to make sure that she was protected. She agreed to do a television interview with Barbara Walters with the understanding that they would not discuss anything political. Betty would gladly discuss herself, Jerry, and life as a mother, but she did not want to risk making any errors when it came to political issues. Walters said Betty's request would be honored and the interview took place with the parameters in place. Walters apparently forgot the rules. Despite the fact that Betty agreed to do the show with the understanding that they would not discuss anything political, it was inevitable. After initial small talk and introductions, the first substantive question to come out of Barbara Walters' mouth was related to the recent Supreme Court ruling in *Roe v. Wade*. There is no way that Barbara Walters could have thought that the ground breaking decision on a woman's right to choose was non-political — Betty had been ambushed. Nevertheless, Betty calmly and politely stated that she agreed with the Court's ruling and that it was about time that we took abortion out of the backwoods and put it into hospitals where it belonged. Betty had stated her position and began to establish herself as a woman of candor. The public was given its first taste of the type of person Betty Ford really was, and the type of public figure she would become.

Even though her response to Walters' question was forthright and honest, the fallout of the Walters interview was immediate — and negative. The general public was not ready for a strong woman who clearly stated her position on controversial issues. Moreover, her position tended to fall to the left of what many would consider appropriate for a member of the Republican Party. However, at the time, the Republican Party was much more moderate and unwilling to interfere in the private lives of citizens. Nevertheless, there were many people who wrote letters stating that Betty had overstepped her bounds and that her position was dangerous.

Dick Cavett and Barbara Walters were not the only interviews that Betty gave. While she was second lady, Betty had reluctantly given a number of interviews — over two hundred writers interviewed her in the first few months — but was never very comfortable in this role. Even though her people were setting the ground rules for any discussions, as the Barbara Walters interview indicates, the protections were never absolute. The interviews were, in Betty's words, "terrifying."[5] She was simply not accustomed to the spotlight and did not relish the thought of letting people into her world. Every time she spoke, she did a wonderful job and never came across as anything but thoughtful and honest. This, however, did not diminish the fact that Betty was not yet comfortable in the spotlight and preferred to stick to her traditional role as mother and CEO of the family. Despite her discomfort (which never showed), the press simply loved her because she made *them* feel comfortable. Years of observing the political arena had paid off.

Betty was a refreshing face for America. The press and the public were used to the "smile but say nothing" approach taken by most politicians' wives. In fact, this was the very approach that Betty had taken for years — until now. She wasn't comfortable, but she wasn't going to shy away either. She talked freely about the children and about herself, and about Jerry. She expressed how the new job was wonderful because it allowed Jerry to be closer to home and not on the road all of the time. Betty also discussed how she and the entire family felt free to criticize Jerry when they felt he was wrong. The press ate it up and were never at a loss for kind things to say about Betty — whether it was about her appearance (some said she had "star" quality) or her demeanor (all were in agreement that she was a very kind, gracious, honest, person).

When she wasn't giving interviews, working with her many charitable groups, or raising the family (which she still did), there was an opportunity for the Fords to do more traveling. Most of this was done in an official capacity, but it was travel nonetheless. Betty represented the administration at the funeral for Martin Luther King, Jr.'s mother who had been shot while playing the organ at church. The president and Jerry were both away so Betty felt that she should go — they agreed. She was beginning to enjoy the freedom that being second lady provided and was starting to forget about any initial misgivings she had about Jerry accepting the new position.

Jerry had been the vice president for less than two weeks when the Senate Watergate Committee served three subpoenas on the White House demanding over five hundred presidential documents and tapes. It seemed that things were heating up and that Richard Nixon was increasingly coming under fire. Jerry thought that the president was innocent and that releasing relevant portions of the tapes could not hurt. Thinking that his role was that of mediator, he expressed his view during a January 6 episode of *Meet the Press*. President Nixon strongly disagreed and chastised Jerry for suggesting that handing over the tapes was a good idea. He was vehemently opposed to giving any of the materials to Congress and that was the end of the discussion. Tension between Jerry and president Nixon began to mount. Jerry believed that the president had done nothing wrong, and wanted to support him, but was not convinced that his actions were in the best interest of either the office or the country. Jerry then discovered that Nixon's speech writers were using him to shield the president — regardless of any damage that it would do to Jerry's reputation. Jerry Ford was getting worried that some of the administration were panicked and he decided to place some distance between himself and the White House. He hired his own speechwriters and brought on Bill Seidman to organize and manage his office. Jerry was increasingly finding himself in a no-win situation.

One Step-Away 73

Every time he publicly supported the president, a new piece of information would come out that made it look like Jerry was part of a cover-up. Jerry was an honest man who loved his country and wanted to do the right thing. He was also a career politician who had a deep respect for the system. Being vice president under Nixon forced him to behave in a manner that he hated. While he had made a career out of taking a firm stand on issues and being honest, he was now zigzagging in front of the press and was continuously contradicting himself. According to Mr. Ford,

> On the one hand, I was chiding Nixon for failing to turn over all the evidence; on the other, I was saying that his attitude was proper. By the nature of the office I held, I was in an impossible situation. I couldn't abandon Nixon, because that would make it appear that I was trying to position myself to become president. Nor could I get too close to him, because if I did I'd risk being sucked into the whirlpool myself. It was a day-by-day balancing act and I detested the whole thing.[6]

He wouldn't have to suffer long.

By the summer of 1974, the only thing on the minds of people across America was Watergate. The scandal had rocked the political system and had raised doubts about government and the individuals that had been elected to represent the people of this country. At the center of this crisis was the President of the United States who many felt had orchestrated the events leading up to Watergate. In July, the House Judiciary Committee voted to impeach the president on three counts. On July 29, the committee voted 27-11 to charge the president with taking part in a criminal conspiracy to obstruct justice in the Watergate investigation. On July 29, they voted 28-10 to charge Nixon with repeatedly failing to carry out his constitutional oath in a series of abuses of power. Finally, on July 30, the committee charged him with the unconstitutional defiance of committee subpoena. Nixon finally handed over the rest of the tapes that he had been ordered to release, but it was too little, too late. An informal poll of House members showed that, if articles of impeachment were presented, both Republicans and Democrats would vote against Nixon. On August 9, 1974, before the House could vote to impeach him, Nixon resigned the presidency, the first incumbent ever to do so.

With the resignation of Nixon, Gerald Ford became the 38th President of the United States. If Agnew's departure, and Jerry's subsequent selection as vice president was a change of plans, the resignation of Richard Nixon put the Fords, — especially Betty, — into a tailspin. The Fords had barely enough time to adjust to the added stress and pressure of the vice-presidency when they were suddenly thrust onto center stage after President Nixon's resignation — Gerald Ford was President of the United States and Betty Ford was the First Lady. Betty Ford was suddenly expected to take on a role that was uncomfortably foreign to her. However, Betty would prove to be a quick study and took to the role of first lady in a way no one had imagined possible.

Chapter 8

A NEW ERA

Gerald Ford was sworn in as the 38th President of the United States on August 9, 1974 and was immediately thrown into an unenviable position. Betty Ford was right there with him. During a brief speech, Jerry talked about how the long national nightmare was over and how it was time to heal the internal wounds of Watergate. He also discussed how he had come into office though unorthodox channels and was therefore not bound by many of the same political promises and campaign platforms that had guided the actions of many of his predecessors. To emphasize his independence, and to reinforce his gratitude to Betty for always being so supportive, he stated, for all of America to hear, "I am indebted to no man and to only one woman, my dear wife." Just as he had done when accepting the vice presidency, Jerry was giving his family, and especially Betty, much deserved credit for his success. As traditional political partnerships, their arrangement was that he would focus on politics and career while she raised the family. If she had not done her part, he would not have succeeded in his. Without Betty Ford, there is no way that Gerald Ford would have been at the podium graciously accepting our nation's highest office.

Being the president is a stressful and taxing position under normal circumstances (if there are ever "normal" circumstances), but August of 1974 was far from normal and Jerry would need Betty's support and understanding more than ever.

Unfortunately, his administration was hampered in its effort to heal America from the very start. In addition to lacking any sort of mandate from the people, since he wasn't elected, Jerry was not given the normal grace period which is granted to incoming presidents. Since he was taking over in the middle of a term, Congress was in place and wasn't undergoing the same transition that the presidency was. In normal situations, the president has about seventy-five days between the time they are elected and the time they take the oath of office. During this time, the president elect can select cabinet members, put together a White House staff, get a sense of their friends and foes in Congress, and decide upon their legislative priorities. This time is crucial for a president in getting off on the right foot. Jerry did not have this luxury. The time between Nixon's resignation (Jerry's "election") and Ford's swearing in ceremony was only a matter of hours — not months.

Gerald Ford entered into a White House that had a number of Nixon holdovers already in place. They felt that Ford's people were relatively amateurish since the "new guard" hadn't had the experience as a presidential administration. The new people, on the other hand, viewed the holdovers as remnants of an administration gone bad that had sent the country into a tailspin. Caught between the two factions, was the new president, Gerald Ford. He needed to rely on the expertise that some of the established people had while, at the same time, transitioning in a new set of people who shared his vision. Given the nature of organizations and the inability of people to embrace change, his was no easy task.

President Ford also had to face many tough substantive issues when he inherited the office from Richard Nixon. The economy was extremely weak with inflation that was accelerating at a rate of over 12 percent per year, shaky market conditions, and the possibility of increased unemployment hanging over the horizon. People were worried about economic conditions at the same time that they didn't feel comfortable with the people entrusted to fix the problem. There were also concerns abroad. Nixon had pulled the United States out of Vietnam, but there were several other areas of potential conflict that could not be ignored. The entire region around Vietnam was still unsettled and tensions were running high. Any conflict threatened to undermine the Paris Peace accords. The middle East was also an area of grave concern. In 1972, the Palestinian Liberation Organization had slaughtered several athletes from Israel during the Olympic Games, and The Yom Kippur War of October 1973 was still a fresh memory. The truce that ended that outbreak, like the Paris Treaty, was in danger of being shattered. We also had the omnipresent tensions between the United States and the Soviet Union. Both nations were in the process of a huge nuclear arms build-up. To top it all off, there had recently been conflict on Cypress that put Greece and Turkey at odds with one another. Peace needed to be restored between these two nations in order to insure the security of the Western Alliance. Needless to say, the new president would need all of the support he could get.

Unlike most vice presidents who ascended into the presidency, Ford could not ride the coat tails of his predecessor. Truman had been able to carry the memory of F.D.R. like a sword. Johnson had been able to use the memory of Kennedy to his advantage as well. They had been able to reassure the people that everything was going to be fine by wrapping themselves in the memory of the departed incumbent. Ford could not wrap himself in Nixon's memory — if anything, he wanted people to forget about Nixon as soon as was humanly possible.

Jerry entered into the office with the understanding that he needed to reestablish faith in the presidency. The years of deceit and scandal that characterized the end of the Nixon administration had left the people feeling disillusioned about the executive branch. Add the recent debacle of Vietnam into the mix, and the entire aura surrounding government as a whole was bad. Americans were basically demoralized, they lacked faith in their elected officials and the institutions of government, and they were looking for a new direction. Ford, realizing that the base of presidential power stems from public support, had to act. He knew that if he could not gain the public's trust, he couldn't get their support for anything else. Without their support, any ideas he had for the future of the country would go nowhere.

He also realized that trust had to come from action and results rather than more empty promises. Previous administrations had made a lot of promises that were never kept — adding to the disillusionment and mistrust. Above all, he needed to provide direction and give America time to heal. He has recounted an old tradition from the American West wherein a "peacestone" was the symbol of triumph. Pioneer families would struggle for years to pay off the mortgage on the family farm. Once the final payment was made, and the property was theirs, they would place a special stone over the fireplace or in the rail post for the stairs. This stone, called the "peacestone," was the symbol that reminded them that the home was theirs at last. Ford saw the turmoil and disarray before him as challenge. In his words, "my ambition was to put the peacestone back in the foundation of America."[1] Unfortunately, he was being hampered by the memory of Nixon hanging over his head. The people of the country viewed him as an extension of the former president — whom they distrusted. His first step was to convince the public that this was, indeed, a new era — Betty would help.

Betty and Jerry both decided that the best approach for them to take would to be as honest, open, and forthright as was possible. The people of America needed to see the first couple as real people and needed to see that the Ford administration was very different than past administrations. In some ways, Nixon actually helped in this regard. By being a very private man who acted in a dictatorial manner, Nixon was a natural contrast to Jerry who was much more of a people person that actively sought the advice of others. Nixon also relished being "the boss" and the way in which he demanded that he be treated was much more formal and royal-like than Jerry would even imagine. It was during the Nixon administration that Arthur Schlesinger coined the term — the "Imperial Presidency." Jerry sought to remove all the trappings of royal treatment. He requested that the Marine band not greet him with "Hail to the Chief," (The University of Michigan fight song would be fine) and he insisted that the living quarters of the White House be called "the residence" rather than "the executive mansion" as Nixon had demanded. Ford also removed all of the electronic listening and recording equipment from the oval office and made sure that the message got out that his was going to be a more "open" administration. He was so intent on changing the presidential image and breaking from Nixon that he even asked the Secret Service to act differently. Under Nixon, the security detail around the president performed their duties in a no-nonsense, grim sort of way. They were even known to be somewhat bullying towards others when it came to doing their job. Ford passed around the word that they were no longer going to push people around simply because they could, and it would be okay (even nice) if they could smile once in a while and appear to be enjoying themselves.

Jerry then set out to ensure that he received a positive image from the press. During his time as vice president, he had given numerous interviews and held close to ninety press conferences. He had tried to be as honest and forthright as possible under his unenviable set of circumstances. He wanted to make sure the press knew that he was going to be honest with them now and he wanted to make sure that there were positive relations between the White House and the White House press corps. In the wake of Watergate and the investigative reporting of Bob Woodward and Carl Bernstein of the Washington Post, such relations were not going to be easy. The press mistrusted public officials more than the public did, and they all wanted to follow in the footsteps of Woodward and Bernstein in uncovering the next great scandal. To smooth the transition, Jerry walked the new chief spokesman for the White House, Jerry terHorst, to the pressroom shortly after he was sworn in. The new spokesman was chosen because he had a firmly established reputation with the Washington press corps and he knew almost all of them on a personal basis. With additions such as terHorst, the administration was on the move.

According to Betty, both she and President Ford were everyday people who came from common middle-class backgrounds. Nevertheless, these common people were thrust into the spotlight during uncommon times. The post-Watergate political environment provided a setting which made an inherently difficult and stressful job even more taxing. Betty had no doubt that her husband would do a wonderful job as president. He had been involved in politics for a very long time and knew the rules of the game. Moreover, Jerry knew most of the people he was going to be dealing with (at least those in Congress). What she wasn't sure about, was her own aptitude for the position. She had been unwillingly thrown into the second ladyship and had barely begun to understand that position. She was now being asked to take on a much more visible "office."

She simply decided that, regardless of the fallout, she would just be herself. In her words, "if they didn't like it, they could kick me out."[2] In doing so, she was reinforcing the entire administration's approach to differentiating themselves from past presidencies. A large part of the differentiation came from them emphasizing that they were simple, common Americans being asked to do a tough job. The "common" background of Mrs. Ford must have instilled in her something special in order for her to survive — in her case flourish — under such circumstances. However, while her background as a dancer, model, professional woman, mother, and congressional wife were all crucial to her development as a person, nothing could adequately prepare her for being first lady.

First and foremost, Betty entered into the office intent on maintaining family relations. To her, family had always been of the utmost importance. Beyond the inherent ties that a mother has with her children, Jerry and Betty were true companions and confidants. President Ford's oath of office provides some insight into the importance of the partnership that the Fords had developed over the years. When he stated that "I am indebted to no man and only to one woman — my dear wife," it became clear that Betty was much more than a social sidekick. She and Mr. Ford had done their best to maintain a normal family life during his years in Congress, and she was not about to see that disappear. While she knew that job pressures would undoubtedly put some strain on the family, and that time would be hard to come by, she set out to maintain stability in any way possible. One seemingly small attempt at normalcy actually created a minor stir when Betty insisted that she and the president would not be sleeping in separate bedrooms and that they would be bringing their own bed into the White House. She was accused of being immoral but didn't care. She was perfectly willing to take on the duties of a first lady but wasn't about to give up part of herself and the things she cared about in the process.

In addition to caring for Jerry and the children, Betty was careful to take care of herself and to keep her sense of humor. Remembering that trying to be superhuman had led to a breakdown, she knew that a balance had to be maintained. She was always conscious of the fact that maintaining her individuality was of vital importance. She brought this philosophy into the White House and it not only helped her, it helped those around her. Just like Jerry, she refused to be treated like royalty. From the very first time she stepped foot into the White House, it was apparent that things were going to be different. She was more relaxed and easy-going than her predecessor had been, and she liked to have fun. She would often put cigarettes in the hands of statues to break up the overly stuffy atmosphere, and had no problem going into the kitchen when she wanted something to eat. In many respects, this was basically the home on Crown View Drive being transplanted to Pennsylvania Avenue. One cannot help but think that the free-spirited Betty Ford had a positive influence on the White House staff by treating them as family and playing ongoing jokes with them. The unpretentious atmosphere created was a breath of fresh air in a troubled time and was very well received. Even visitors noticed that the new administration was very different. As ex-Beatle George Harrison put it, after a visit to the Fords' new home, "I feel good vibes about this White House."

Life was not all fun and games, however. Betty also realized that the office required a certain seriousness (in public) and that the citizenry was scrutinizing the entire Ford administration (the first lady included). Mrs. Ford was placed center stage and was asked to perform without time to truly prepare. How did she do it? Mrs. Ford firmly believed that the best way to deal with public matters was to avoid skirting issues and to be as honest as possible. Having spent a number of years in Washington prior to assuming the office of first lady, Mrs. Ford had friends and role models who had preceded her. From their experiences, she knew that there would be press conferences, questions, and constant attention. It was decided from the outset that her approach to the office of the first lady would be similar to that of Jerry's approach to the presidency — it would be direct. In discussing her view on the position of first lady Mrs. Ford has stated that, "my approach was, I will just be open and not beat around the bush and answer their questions as best I can."[3] The Ford presidency came at a time when the citizenry was questioning the integrity of government and Mrs. Ford believed that candor and honesty from the first lady would be as crucial to the healing process as candor and honesty out of the oval office. Such an approach wasn't especially difficult since it was in her nature. However, her openness was enhanced by the fact that she knew most of the press members personally. While never fully at ease in the spotlight, all of the years spent in and around Washington had allowed Mrs. Ford to cultivate relationships with the press. The brief time as second lady had given her some opportunity to "practice," so when thrust in front of reporters as the first lady she was able to appear comfortable dealing with them and had no trouble telling them the truth.

Even with personal relationships in place, however, the candor initially caught many media persons off-guard. They knew that Betty was an honest person, but they had never really experienced a first lady who was as open as Betty. This is not to suggest that they were unhappy. According to Mrs. Ford, "it was not what they expected and I think they were not only surprised but they were pleased. I didn't know how it was going to come out [the honest approach], but I felt I got good grades on that." Good grades indeed! The media loved her! According to one *Washington Post* columnist at the time, "she is too honest. Mrs. Ford wears her defect like diamonds. And they dazzle."

Both she and Jerry would need to continue to "dazzle" the media and the American public in their quest for closure after Watergate. They needed to clearly establish themselves and their agenda for moving America forward to better times. It was a new era.

Chapter 9

THE SYMBOLIC ROLE

The president really serves as both chief executive and chief of state. As chief executive, he (eventually she) is asked to run the country and represent it. As the head of state, the president serves in a largely symbolic capacity — the symbolic head of the nation. When presidents receive foreign dignitaries, the first lady is often right there beside him. Moreover, first ladies have often met some of these dignitaries on their own, have traveled to other nations to serve as America's "queen," and have attended any number of formal functions as one of our nation's symbols.

In their symbolic roles, the Fords were able to do a great deal of traveling. If not for the presidency, Betty would not have been exposed to the wide range of cultures that the world has to offer. Some of the trips were whirlwind tours that left little time for personal enjoyment — such as the time they shuttled from Brussels, to Madrid, to Salzburg, and then on to Rome in a condensed period of time. Others were much more relaxed and memorable. Betty has recalled the overwhelming welcome that they received from General Franco in Spain. They were treated to a very elegant state dinner and got to enjoy the company of both Franco and the future leader of Spain, Prince Juan Carlos.

Less than two months after the trip to Spain, the Fords were off to Eastern Europe and a five country visit (over only a nine day period) of Poland, Yugoslavia, West Germany, Finland, and Romania. Unfortunately for Betty, she got sick during the trip and even had to excuse herself from the state dinner in Romania. Fortunately, this was the last leg of the trip and she didn't have to suffer for very long. She was able to go home to the White House and get some rest — for four weeks.

They then embarked for a tour of the East with stops in China, Indonesia, and Manila.

In China, Betty went to visit some museums and a dance school. At the school, Betty got caught up in the moment and sort of relived her past. Despite the fact that she suffered from arthritis and a pinched nerve, and despite the fact that she hadn't really done ballet for quite some time, she took off her shoes and went *en point*. A photographer captured the moment and the picture of Betty, arms outstretched amidst her Chinese hosts portrayed one of our symbolic leaders doing her part to cement relations between two troubled countries. After the picture hit the papers, and the corresponding story hailed her as being better than the diplomats at making peace, Betty told Jerry they could go home — that the world was safe now.

The trip ended in Manila where the Fords were greeted by one hundred thousand cheering Filipinos. Imelda Marcos, wife of then president, Ferdinand Marcos, had feared that the Fords would not be treated well in China (of course, she had been wrong — then again, she hadn't counted on Betty's charm) and wanted them to received a memorable welcome. She managed to turn out a large segment of the population, from all nationalities, dressed in their native costumes and playing musical instruments. The welcoming committee ended up being a nine-mile parade that lined the avenue all the way from the airport to the presidential palace. It was far more impressive than any red carpet. Just as Betty and Jerry were in Manila to represent the United States, Mrs. Marcos was acting as a representative of the Philippines and she wanted to leave a lasting mark.

One of the primary "duties" of being the first lady is to serve as the symbolic hostess for the country. This aspect of the first ladyship has been a traditional component from the very beginning. In fact, several of Betty Ford's predecessors, such as Dolly Madison, established their solid reputations by being gracious hostesses.

Almost immediately after Jerry was sworn in, Betty was asked to perform in her newly acquired symbolic capacity. It was August 10, 1974, and Betty was informed that she would be hosting the King of Jordan very soon. She was still at home in Virginia when a White House aide called to ask about her plans for the upcoming state dinner. When Betty asked, "what state dinner?" the aide informed her that King Hussein would be attending a state dinner in less than one week — on the 16th. Betty was caught completely off guard because she didn't know anything about the visit. Nevertheless, she jumped right in and began to make plans for her first state dinner as the new first lady. She enlisted the help of a friend (Peggy Stanton, a congressman's wife) to help her prepare the guest list, and between the two of them, they managed to pull it off.

The Symbolic Role   85

Fortunately for Betty and Jerry, they had both hosted King Hussein during their time as second couple. Meeting the King at the State Department made it so that Betty wasn't quite as nervous about the upcoming dinner as she might have normally been. Besides, there were a large number of well-prepared White House employees who were veterans when it came to putting on lavish dinners. With people in place to do the cooking, cleaning, baking, and just about anything a person could ask for, Betty simply needed to decide what she wanted. The only thing Betty had to worry about was meeting Queen Alia. King Hussein was a nice man and Betty felt comfortable around him, but she had never met the Queen and she didn't want to make a poor impression.

Since Jerry and Betty weren't yet staying at the White House, they had to drive up from Alexandria to meet their guests for dinner. Normally, special guests will stay at the White House with the president and first lady, but this was one more example of how the Ford presidency was not normal. Despite the inconvenience of meeting up at the White House, the dinner went well. Betty remembers, from a carefully kept scrapbook of her time in office, that they all dined on cold salmon, roast beef, artichoke salad, Brie, and mousse. They also danced, talked, and had a wonderful time. Betty had made it through her first state dinner — although the Queen would later tell her that she'd had doubts. Everything went well, but Betty had been so nervous that Queen Alia didn't know if she would last the evening.

After the state dinner for the King and Queen of Jordan, Betty would have notice for future events. As mentioned, she would not have to plan these events alone. At the time she took over as first lady, there were roughly twenty-five staff members working for her — from Nancy Howe who had been with her for a number of months as personal assistant, to Lucy Winchester, the social secretary that had served under Pat Nixon. She kept Nancy, but replaced all of the holdovers. The first two people to be replaced were Lucy Winchester and Helen Smith, the press secretary for Pat Nixon. Betty thought both of the women were nice and capable but she, like Jerry, needed to make a clean break with the former administration and make an imprint of their own. Besides, Betty had a vision for the way things should be done and these two women were stuck in the old way of doing things. For example, as Betty began to plan more state dinners, Lucy and her aides would tell Betty how they were to be done. It wasn't really posed as suggestion but more of a turf battle. Betty inwardly thought that perhaps the way that Lucy did things was not the way that she wanted to do them. Since they didn't seem to share the vision, and Betty was the boss, they parted company. Betty has said that it was a simple parting of company with no hard feelings. The bottom line is that Betty fired her. Betty fired Helen Smith too.

Smith had arranged for Betty to go to Chicago to make her first big speech as part of a fund raising activity for Republican women (part of the symbolic role the first lady plays and a part of the campaign role that the first lady plays which will be discussed in a later chapter). Since it was her first major speech, Betty was nervous. Ms. Smith assured Betty that she wouldn't have to face any reporters or deal with any distractions until the event was over. However, on the plane to Chicago, Betty found herself surrounded by reporters. She couldn't ignore them and the whole trip was something of a fiasco for Betty. She, for obvious reasons, was not happy with her press secretary. Only about one week into the job, Betty was looking for a new press secretary. The day after the state dinner with the King and Queen of Jordan, Betty interviewed Sheila Rabb Weidenfeld while sitting in her Crown View Drive home. Wiedenfeld, a television producer, had no experience in politics but liked what she saw in Betty. Weidenfeld accepted the position and stayed with Betty through the entire Ford administration.

With new staff, Betty was prepared to handle the press and any foreign dignitaries that might come her way — and come they did. Betty learned how to throw a good party! Not many people understand the behind the scenes planning that goes into White House social affairs — there are the obvious staff people such as the social secretary (basically a party planner) and a number of lesser known, but valuable, assistants. The White House even employs social aides who are escorts. The aides are trained in the proper way to escort a man or woman and are skilled at helping guests to feel comfortable and welcome. Betty took full advantage of all the staff at her disposal and held weekly meetings with the ushers, tour guides, various secretaries, and even the social aides.

Since Betty had to serve as a symbol for our country, she wanted to do it well. She planned guest lists based on the people the honorees would most enjoy. In doing so, she also tried to bring in a representation of America's best and brightest from all areas. She brought in actors, musicians, doctors, and even labor leaders. She wanted to show her guests what "Americans" were like. She was able to use the state dinners as a showcase for the country — that is a basic part of the hostess and symbolic roles played by the first lady.

Betty even went out of her way to come up with unique programs and menus that would give the guests something to remember. The guests almost always liked what Betty arranged — even if some of the Washington social columnists and food critics thought that Betty had done poorly. She learned that, while she was a symbol for *all* of America, there was simply no pleasing everyone. She did the best she could and focused on her guests rather than her critics.

In her hostess capacity, Betty was able to meet and entertain some very interesting and influential people. Among her favorites, at least her most

The Symbolic Role   87

memorable, included state dinners for Queen Elizabeth, Egyptian President Anwar Sadat, President Kekkonen of Finland, Foreign Minister Cosgrave of Ireland, President Walter Scheel of the Federal Republic of Germany, and The Emperor and Empress of Japan.

One of the most fun, and inventive, evenings was the state dinner thrown for Egyptian President Anwar Sadat. Betty knew that Sadat was a big fan of the American West. Anything having to do with cowboys and the West simply made Sadat feel at ease. Betty decided to throw a state dinner with a western theme. One of the advantages to being the first lady and hosting events at the White House is that people and institutions are sometimes willing to lend items for display. Betty was able to get the Eamon Carter Museum in Dallas-Fort Worth to donate a number of C.M. Russell and Charles Remmington bronzes. Russell and Remmington are perhaps the two most famous of the "Cowboy Artists," so getting their work donated was really something special. Betty placed the bronzes around the room and used some of the smaller sculptures as centerpieces on the tables. It was really quite a sight. The use of art for centerpieces was also a great way to start conversations at the tables.

Keeping with the western theme, Betty had tried to get country western singer, Johnny Cash, to sing. Unfortunately, Cash got sick and they had to rush to come up with a back up plan. They managed to get jazz singer and show performer, Pearl Bailey, to fly down between shows in Boston. While it wasn't exactly keeping with the western theme, it was fortunate that Betty managed to get a hold of Pearl Bailey. Betty was just trying to find an entertainer, but Bailey was held in high regard by President Sadat who had once given her one of Egypt's highest honors.

Bailey was full of energy and turned out to be the life of the party. She took off the vice president's glasses so she could read the lyrics to a song she wanted to sing for Omar Sharif. Sharif was a famous actor and he also happened to be Egyptian — an obvious guest for the Sadat dinner. She sang to Sharif and tried to get him to dance. When he refused, she "settled" for the Egyptian president. Sadat must have really like Bailey since he had never danced before. Betty's parties brought out the best in people. Bailey ended the evening by running after Sadat's limousine trying to give him President Ford's pipe. (Someone had told her it belonged to the president — she didn't ask which one). Everyone had a wonderful time with the western evening turned Pearl Bailey night.

Not all of the events were as casual as was the western theme event thrown for Anwar Sadat. There were times when Betty thought it best to be more formal, for example dinners thrown for the Queen of England and the Shah of Iran. The Emperor and Empress of Japan were also privy to a formal affair. This was the first trip to America by reigning Japanese monarchs and Betty wanted to present them with a grand affair. Suspecting that the Emperor and Empress were accustomed to finery, Betty and the staff pulled out the best linen, the silver candlesticks surrounded with flower blossoms, and the best china and table settings the White House had to offer. Of course, everyone was in white tie and tails — very proper and formal as would befit the Japanese monarchs. As it turns out, they were actually more interested in finding out more of the relaxed, informal customs of Americans. This was one time that Betty had misread the guests. Nevertheless, the guests rose to the occasion and arrived dressed in splendid fashion. The event was a success, despite the formality.

Another very formal affair was arranged for the Queen of England. The Queen and Prince Phillip were making quite a stir in America and they were the talk of the nation. This meant that the State Department had its hands full and was trying desperately to manage the royal couple while they were in this country. They were making so many engagements and commitments for the Queen and her husband that Betty finally had to intervene on their behalf. She called General Scowcroft of the National Security Council and told him that the White House visit would be handled by her staff without any State Department involvement. They could send over a staff liaison, but that was the most she would allow — she was stern when she wanted or needed to be. With that settled, she set about planning for the event.

Since this was going to be a very grand occasion, Betty decided that they should hold the dinner outdoors. This would serve three purposes. First, it was a beautiful setting outside in the rose garden. Second, holding the event outdoors would allow them to have an expanded guest list. Since this was going to be a very high profile visit, they didn't want to limit the number of people in attendance. Dining inside generally limited the guest list to around 150 and they thought that they might want to invite more. Finally, holding the event outside would free up the rest of the White House during the height of tourist season. Not only does the first lady serve as a symbol, but the White House itself is a symbol which Betty did not want to close. By holding the state dinner under a large tent, decorated so that it was really just a large outdoor room, the White House could remain open for visitors while they prepared for the Queen's arrival.

Despite the outdoor setting, Betty and the staff managed to create a very royal atmosphere. They had violinists stationed on the path to the outdoor room and having the combination of formality with the gorgeousness of open night air made for a very impressive atmosphere. Of course, the guest list was equally impressive. Betty was able to get some of the Queen's favorite actors such as Bob Hope and Telly Savalas to attend, and the event went off without any trouble.

The Symbolic Role

89

Betty even managed to throw some American "pop culture" into the mix — much to the Queen's delight. Although the dinner was a very formal affair, Betty had arranged for the pop sensation Captain and Tennille to perform that evening. While protocol probably would have required that they not sing "Muskrat Love," the Queen loved it. She was, after all, human.

Given her past, it should be of no surprise that dancing played a part in most of the state dinners thrown by Betty Ford (the former dancer). Three of Betty's best stories related to White House dancing involve a lost opportunity, a bad experience, and a case of presidential stubbornness. Her lost opportunity came when Fred Astaire was one of the guests at a state dinner. While there were many big-name stars in attendance, Betty was drawn to Mr. Astaire — he was the artist. She dreamed about twirling around the floor with one of America's most famous dancers but he said that ballroom dancing was not really his thing. She would not give in, and he finally relented. Unfortunately, as the song was about to begin, duty called. President Ford had come over to inform her that the guests of honor were leaving. She was torn — she had a job to do, but she *really* wanted to dance with Fred Astaire. Her loyalty to job, husband, and country won out and she left for a short time. When she returned, the opportunity had passed. Astaire was dancing with another woman and Betty had a hard time even getting close to him again. She never did get to dance with him.

Her bad experience came when she was forced to dance with a person who was clearly not as fleet of foot as Fred Astaire. In fact, President Kekkonen of Finland probably seemed to have feet made of stone. He was a tall man who was very heavy on his feet. Betty had always made it a practice to dance with as many guests as possible — especially the guests of honor. Unfortunately, dancing with President Kekkonen was hard work. Betty has even said that dancing with him was like jogging. In other words, it was a real workout. One of their staff members, Bob Barrett, was watching the encounter with the Fords' daughter, Susan. They both had a great time watching Betty struggle. When they finished, the president asked Susan to dance. Barrett tried to cut in and save Susan from the agony but Betty wouldn't let him — she had done it and now it was Susan's turn. That would teach her to laugh at her poor mother when she was in obvious distress.

President Ford had an opportunity to feel distressed on the dance floor too. He loved to dance to old big band music but had a hard time finding the groove to much of anything else. During a state dinner held in honor of Foreign Minister Cosgrave of Ireland, Jerry found himself out on the dance floor with Mrs. Cosgrove. The band started belting out a fairly modern jazz tune that left Jerry feeling somewhat awkward. When Mr. Cosgrove requested a jig, things went from bad to worse for the president. Jerry was getting very frustrated and reportedly called Bob Barrett over to say, "if they won't play some music I can dance to, I'm just not going to come to these things any more."[1] Betty thought that Jerry pouting and threatening to avoid state dinners was pretty funny.

Regardless of Betty's glee, Barrett went to the bandleader and told him that the president wanted some big band music. The band leader was a bit indignant and stated that he'd been playing at state dinners for over ten years and that he knew what he was doing. Barrett, not wanting to face the frustrated Jerry, told the band leader that he could either play what the primary occupant of the White House wanted — and play inside the White House — or he could play whatever he wanted ... outside. The bandleader acquiesced. Jerry was still sulking at the end of the night because he was the president and he wanted music he could dance to. Jerry rarely let things get to him, but this time it was almost like the little boy who wanted to take his marbles and go home.

Dancing stories and dinner plans aside, Betty and Jerry were able to invite a large number of talented and interesting people to their dinner parties. Among those who would find their way to the White House while Betty was first lady was a virtual "who's who" of Hollywood, politics, music, and industry. Guests included Warren Beatty, Cary Grant, Kirk Douglas, Beverly Sills, Dionne Warwick, George Harrison, and many others. The success was due to both the careful planning that went into each event by Betty and her staff and to Betty herself. She was very careful to monitor how things were going and was always on the lookout for ways to make each guest feel welcome and at ease. When the White House threw a party, Betty Ford went to work. In her words, "I try to keep an eye on how the party is going. I try to see if anything needs to be done, without being rude to the person I'm talking to. I glance fast from the corner of my eye, and then I get right back to the conversation. Most of all I want to project an easy feeling at our parties."[2] She was able to make people feel very much at ease. Betty's parties became a thing of legend around Washington and people were dying to get invited. When invitations were issued, acceptance was high and regrets were few.

Occasionally they would host parties to honor those in and around Washington. Dinners to honor congressmen, senators, and judges helped to keep the machine of government oiled. One particular dinner, however, provides a perfect segue into a chapter on Betty Ford's issues and causes. In this case, the Fords were hosting a judiciary dinner that would be attended by federal judges from all over the country. There was about to be an opening on the Supreme Court and one of the guests would most likely be named as a replacement for the retiring Justice Douglas. Betty had been lobbying very hard for Jerry to name a woman to the Court. The struggle for equal rights and the elevation of women into key positions in government was Betty's greatest cause. She had worked on Jerry to push the Equal Rights Amendment to a vote when he was in Congress and she wasn't going to let up now. She actually thought he was considering naming a woman until they were preparing for the judiciary dinner. While dressing, Jerry let it slip that the man he was going to name would be at the dinner that evening — it was the first time she had heard his intentions and the first time she learned that a woman would not be in the cards. While disappointed, she knew that there would be other opportunities to advance the cause of women. She continued to dress and gamely went out to be the wonderful hostess and symbol of government that she always was.

Chapter 10

BETTY'S CAUSES

Nobody really expected Mrs. Ford to make any kind of mark in her husband's presidency. In fact, as a gesture of good will, a holdover from the Nixon staff created a list of "appropriate activities" for the new first lady to follow — a list which included such benign activities as entertaining disabled veterans and the handicapped, providing interviews to women's magazines, planning fashion shows, and teaching Sunday school in the White House. Despite the low expectations and her tendency to be ill-at-ease with the press, a number of occurrences early in the Ford presidency made Betty aware of the potential for influence she held as first lady. Even with the tremendous outpouring of mail in the wake of the Barbara Walters interview (most of it negative), Betty had failed to realize the full magnitude of her position. However, after her first press conference as first lady, the power she held slowly began to dawn on her. This press conference marked a critical series of events that truly helped shape Betty Ford from a soft-spoken, somewhat camera shy congressional wife into one of the most outspoken, powerful first ladies of the modern era — a woman whose social and political influence was unheard of for the times.

THE PRESS CONFERENCE AND SUPPORT FOR EQUAL RIGHTS

A seemingly innocent press conference held early in the Ford presidency marked the beginning of Betty Ford's movement towards social and political activism. Despite the fact that this was the first formal press conference held by a first lady since 1952, there was little reason to believe that Mrs. Ford was going to have any goals that carried even a hint of controversy. As she outlined her plans, the press corps' expectations appeared to be confirmed. She began by stating that she intended to focus on promoting programs for underprivileged and mentally challenged children. She also stated that she intended to concentrate on attaining greater support for the arts (something which was only natural given her background as a dancer). These were two very uncontroversial topics which, by themselves, would have been very much in line with the traditional role of the first lady. Then, Betty dropped the bomb — she told reporters she favored greater political participation by women, she reiterated her support of the Supreme Court ruling on abortion, and she planned on using her office to work towards ratification of the Equal Rights Amendment (ERA).

The Equal Rights Amendment was the idea of a woman named Alice Paul who was the head of the National Women's Party in the early 1920's. It was this same group that was at the forefront of the suffrage movement to gain back the right for women to vote. Paul convinced Senator Curtis and Representative Anthony (nephew of famous suffragette, Susan B. Anthony) to introduce the ERA to Congress in 1923. From 1923 to 1970, Paul was instrumental in getting the measure reintroduced with each new Congress — only to see it languish in committee. In 1967, The National Organization for Women (NOW) was formed and pledged to fight for passage of the ERA. In 1970 the measure was finally pulled out of committee and debates on the measure began — culminating in the 1971 passage by the House and the 1972 passage by the Senate. The measure they passed was relatively simple, yet highly contentious. It really had only three main sections:

sect. 1   Equality of rights under the law shall not be denied or abridged by the United States or by any State on account of sex.

sect. 2   The Congress shall have the power to enforce, by appropriate legislation, the provisions of this article.

sect. 3   This amendment shall take effect two years after the date of ratification

There was, however, a time limit. When the Congress passed the measure and placed it in the hands of the states for ratification as a constitutional amendment, they included a sunset provision. If the ERA was not ratified by the required 3/4 of the states within seven years, it would be a dead issue. This was what Betty was fighting for.

The amount of press that Betty received after announcing her support for the Equal Rights Amendment, coupled with an increasing number of letters, began to reveal that people were listening. Over time, as Betty became more and more involved with the ERA, the amount of mail increased dramatically. Betty was actually perceived by anti-ERA forces as being such a threat that Phyllis Schafly of "STOP ERA" requested that Betty provide an accounting of how much federal money was being spent on the endorsement — either through telephone bills, staff time, or salaries of other federal officials working on the issue. At the time of the initial press conference, however, the influence that Betty wielded was only beginning to develop and she was only marginally aware of her potential power.

The role that Betty Ford actually played in the fight for women's rights is often underplayed. However, when it came to supporting the Equal Rights Amendment, she was a vocal advocate and a strong lobbying force. Even before moving into an actual position such as the first or second lady, Betty had been an active lobbyist around the house on Crown View Drive. Jerry might have been supportive of the ERA on his own, but Betty made sure that he actively supported the measure. Betty was so persuasive that Jerry actually lined up enough Republican votes to pass the amendment through Congress. Moreover, it was Gerald Ford who persuaded fellow Michigan representative, Martha Griffiths (a Democrat) to file a discharge petition so that the measure could get out of the House Judiciary Committee where it had been resting for forty-seven years.

As first lady, Betty made speeches in support of the ERA, openly discussed equal rights for women in interviews, and even contacted legislators across the country encouraging them to vote for the Amendment — and if they couldn't openly endorse the measure, she wanted them to at least allow it to come to a vote. Schaffly's vision that Betty could be a force was correct and she again called for an accounting of her actions. Not to be dissuaded, Mrs. Ford carried on and pushed forward with true style. She even had an ERA flag (designed by one of her Secret Service detail) placed on her car. She had jokingly mentioned that the president and other dignitaries had flags but she didn't — she had a car but no flag. She said, "If the president gets flags, why shouldn't the first lady?" What better way to announce *her* motorcade than with a bright red, white, and blue flag emblazoned with ERA?

Cancer and Being a Role Model

One event can be seen as a turning point in Betty Ford's political life. It was also an emotional and pivotal point in the lives of the entire Ford family. The date of this event was September 26, 1974 — the day Betty Ford was diagnosed with breast cancer.

The date was one of pure coincidence, as Betty hadn't intended to go the doctor's office at all. Her personal assistant, Nancy Howe, was scheduled to see her physician and Betty decided to go along. Since it was around the time for her six month gynecological check-up, Betty decided to have herself examined. When a tumor was discovered, Betty and the rest of the Fords were in shock. Despite the very private nature of the situation, Betty made an important decision that would have a tremendous social impact — she decided to make her condition known to the public. While she could have quietly had the tumor removed and gone on with her life as if nothing had happened, Betty decided to discuss the uncomfortable issue of breast cancer and her ensuing mastectomy. While such a decision was undoubtedly difficult, Betty, being a very unassuming person, acted as if she had no choice at all. According to her, "I got a lot of credit for having gone public with my mastectomy, but if I hadn't been the wife of the President of the United States, the press would not have come racing after my story, so in a way it was fate."[1] She adds, "there had been so much cover-up during Watergate that we wanted to be sure there would be no cover-up in the Ford administration. So rather than continue this traditional silence about breast cancer, we felt we had to be very public."[2] These are very modest statements which tend to underplay the heroics of Betty's decision and the impact that the decision had on her career, the public, and the issue of breast cancer.

By going public with her cancer and mastectomy, Betty Ford was personally responsible for increased awareness. After Betty went public to alert as many women as possible to the benefits of early detection, millions of women scheduled appointments at breast cancer clinics across the country. According to columnist Lisa Liebman, "her courage and candor not only removed the stigma from the topic but also saved countless lives."[3] (Among the lives saved was Happy Rockefeller, the vice president's wife, who underwent a mastectomy shortly after Betty).

Physicians still refer to the "Betty Ford effect" and the number of diagnosed cases directly attributable to her speaking out.

The response was overwhelming and the letters poured in — much more so than after both her famous interview with Barbara Walters and her first press conference. This time, however, nearly all of the letters were positive. Betty received over 55,000 cards and letters from women who had mastectomies or who were encouraged by Betty's experience to get check-ups. From the standpoint of shaping her attitude towards the Office of First Lady, the response was critical. For the first time, Betty truly understood the extraordinary power she held. According to Mrs. Ford, "I'd come to recognize more clearly the power of the woman in the White House. Not *my* power, but the power of the position, a power which could be used to help."[4] Once again, words of modesty, as Betty Ford was beginning to be able to use the power like few had before her. She began to evolve into the first lady she would become and the transformation was not lost on those around her. According to her son, Jack, the experience allowed Betty to break from the past and focus more towards the future as a woman, with a vision, in a position to make things happen. In his words,

> She could have just sat around feeling sorry for herself, or been very hush-hush about it. But she decided to bring it all out in the open, to tell it like it is. I think that's when she truly realized she had her own identity, when she told the whole country about her illness and shared this intimate thing. It's a funny connection, but I think the way she spoke up about her illness was responsible for her strong support of the Equal Rights Amendment. She finally became her own person.[5]

While she was making the transition into being a very influential public figure, and she was devoting time to very serious social concerns, Betty never lost touch with the other areas that mattered to her. Two of these areas were working for children and, of course, maintaining her family.

Helping Children

Upon entering into the office of first lady, Mrs. Ford was asked about her "program." She replied that she didn't really have a program but that she had a number of interests that she planned to pursue. Among these interests were the arts and placing more attention on the neglected segments of society whom she felt were generally mistreated — primarily the elderly, the poor, and children with disabilities. Although she had no "program," Mrs. Ford attacked these issues with vigor and ended up addressing them all. Mrs. Ford had a particular fondness for the arts, especially for dance. As first lady, she had various people from the arts and humanities invited to the White House and fought for increased funding for the National Endowment for the Arts. Mrs. Ford even convinced President Ford to bestow the Presidential Medal of Freedom on her old dance instructor, Martha Graham — the first dancer ever to receive the prestigious honor.

Betty had begun to work for a number of causes such as Goodwill Industries and fine arts (especially promotion of the Art Train) while she was second lady. However, as she recognized the power of the White House, much of her attention was diverted to helping children — especially those who were disabled, sick, abused, and orphaned. One of her biggest causes was to assist with the Washington Hospital for Sick Children. This institution was different than the more publicized Children's Hospital but it served a very real need. Most of the children were minority and all were either severely injured or mentally challenged. One child had a particularly lasting impact on Mrs. Ford — an infant who had been burned by having lit cigarettes pressed into her ears because her father had grown tired of her crying. Other children were basically dropped off by their families to be forgotten. The families didn't want to be burdened by the hardships that go with raising disabled children. Betty would spend hours sitting with the children and giving them the attention they longed for and so richly deserved. Ultimately, Betty did more for the hospital than just give the children some of her precious time. She worked to get business people to make donations to the hospital. One of her friends, New York businessman Milton Hoffman, even donated two new rooms for the hospital. One was named after his wife and the other was named after Betty. Beyond the Washington Hospital for Sick Children, Betty worked for a group called "No Greater Love," which helped the children of soldiers lost or missing in action. She also got involved with cancer and arthritis foundations and posed with children for Easter Seals and Multiple Sclerosis fund raising campaigns. Anything she could do to help, she would do. The passion she had for children's causes really should have come as no surprise. She had helped children when she was younger, and she was the mother of four. Seeing how fragile some of these youngsters were really helped to reinforce for her how precious her own children were and how important her family was to her life.

The Importance of Family

Betty never lost sight of the fact that she was a mother long before she was the first lady.

It could be said that her family was her biggest cause. She always fought to preserve and cherish her children and her husband. Earlier in life, she was so devoted to them that she lost herself. While she had really found herself as first lady, she never forgot about the family and its importance.

Betty changed the rules when it came to the president and first lady sleeping in separate bedrooms. They were a couple, and America would just have to live with that. They also remodeled Air Force One, that had traditionally been partitioned off for the president to have an individual work space. She and Jerry had always shared a home and they would continue to cohabitate even when he was the President of the United States. Power and office were not going to influence the way they interacted and the way that they led their lives when out of the public eye. Betty was determined to not allow the presidency to change any of the family interactions and dynamics that they had worked so hard to develop over the years.

Although they were famous, they were constantly in the spotlight, and there was the ever-present secret service detail, Betty wanted her children to be able to live their lives in a somewhat normal fashion. This meant that she would allow them to become their own people with her support. This meshed with the view shared by both she and President Ford — that they did not possess their children. They believed that the children were merely loaned to them to raise to the best of their ability and that they could not, and should not, *control* and manage them. At times, this led to some comments in the press that might not correspond with Jerry's political views. Rather than lash out for the damage it may have caused, he would say that they were entitled to their own opinions and views, even if he disagreed with them.

The Ford support network was very strong. Even Jerry's decision to try for the minority leader post had been sealed by his son saying, "go for it Dad." That was not the first or last time that they had all consulted one another. When asked if there was a partnership between she and Jerry, Betty replied, "You're right. We always say in many ways it was a partnership with our children too." The children were allowed to participate in substantive discussions, were educated on Jerry's position and goals, and were encouraged to freely contribute or criticize.

Jack became one of Jerry's self-appointed critics. He called his father to comment that an "informal" address to the nation from the White House library was clearly staged and that it was not in his father's character to try and deceive anyone. Jack went so far as to tell his father that the obvious break from character was an embarrassment to him as a son. Jerry took the comments to heart and the staged look disappeared from future TV appearances.

The children didn't always agree, but this too was encouraged. Dialogue was thought to be healthy. Mike felt free to comment on more substantive areas — such as his father's decision to pardon former President Richard Nixon. Jerry thought it was necessary for the nation to heal quicker. He wanted to put the whole Watergate episode behind them as quickly as possible. Mike, on the other hand, told members of the press that Richard Nixon owed the public a full and "total confession" about his role in the fiasco. Jerry's response, in keeping with the on-going support for independent thought, was "all my children have spoken for themselves since they first learned to speak, and not always with my approval. I expect that to continue."[6] Jack, generally the critic, agreed with his father on this one. He felt that it was a tough trade off for his father to make — moral right and wrong versus doing what was best for the country. Without the pardon, Nixon would have been testifying for months and the shame brought on the presidency would have been extended for a long time. Besides, for a person who wanted to be president badly enough to commit criminal acts, losing the office was probably the ultimate punishment.

Maintaining the ability to civilly disagree, even in the press, was part of keeping the family together. They trusted one another and loved one another. They were the strongest support that each could have — even in disagreement. If individuality was shut down simply because they were under more intense media scrutiny, everything that Betty and Jerry had worked so hard to instill in their children would have been lost. The nucleus that was so important for Betty would have been destroyed. This nucleus would be even more important, and the support even more critical, if they were all to decide that Jerry should run for re-election.

Chapter 11

ELECTION HOPES

Gerald R. Ford was sworn in as the 38th President of the United States on August 9, 1974 — a day which Betty Ford has described as "the saddest day of my life."[1] Part of the sadness stemmed from the fact that the Fords and Nixons were friends. She was particularly fond of Pat Nixon whom she thought was a "very warm, friendly person."[2] Betty, being a caring person herself, hated seeing the pain and agony going on in the White House as the Nixons were in hiding, sealed off in isolation from the media and the rest of the world. Of the protests going on outside, Betty felt that the personal attacks against Pat were particularly cruel and unfair. The remainder of the sadness of August 9th found its roots in fear, nervousness, and apprehension.

Although she was initially fearful and reluctant, Betty had found that she enjoyed the position. The parties and the interesting people allowed her to live something of a fantasy existence. It really was a fairy tale come to life. She also like the traveling she was able to do in her symbolic role as one of the nation's figure heads. Most of all, however, she had really begun to make a difference. She was able to be herself and carve out her own identity — which was something seriously lacking while she was a congressman's wife. In doing so, she was also able to make a huge difference in the lives of others and was able to make some inroads into those areas that mattered the most to her — especially women's rights and the ERA. In short, apprehension and fear had given way to love and respect. Her saddest day had turned into some of her proudest moments.

Betty, despite the fact that she and Jerry had once pointed to 1977 as their retirement year, wanted to stay in the White House. Jerry wanted to stay too. He still had a number of issues that mattered to him. He was also just getting into the flow of things and was feeling like he understood the office a bit better. Jerry felt that he could still get some things accomplished. With this in mind, they embarked on a campaign that would, perhaps, allow Jerry to actually be elected to office. As with everything, this would be a family affair.

Since Jerry had promised to retire in January of 1977, he was fully prepared to live up to his obligation and not seek re-election. Betty knew he wanted to stay on, and the children knew he wanted to stay on, but they hadn't given him the okay. Finally, in typical Ford fashion, a family decision released Jerry from his retirement promise and he was given the go ahead to seek the Republican nomination for president in 1976. He made an official announcement on July 8, 1975.

When he was placed into the presidency, he was fully aware of the unique circumstances and the fact that he had not been elected — even to the vice presidency. In the inaugural address following his swearing in as Nixon's replacement he looked at America and stated, "I am acutely aware that you have not elected me as your president by your ballots, so I ask that you confirm me as your president with your prayers." On July 8, 1975, he was basically saying he would be asking them to confirm him with their votes the following year. It would not be an easy year.

The Betty Ford that most people remember was comfortable with her views and at ease in discussing them during August of 1975. The nation had a first lady who had independent thoughts and felt confident enough in herself to express her opinion. Her stand on ERA had been firmly established, her position on abortion was well known, and she had become the champion for women with breast cancer across the nation. Betty Ford was on a roll and her popularity was unprecedented. For much of the Ford presidency, Betty enjoyed higher ratings than her husband Jerry. Nothing, however, could have braced the nation for the honesty Betty would display during an interview for the CBS evening show, *60 minutes*.

During an interview with Morley Safer, broadcast August 10, 1975, Betty was asked about various controversial social and political issues such as equal rights, abortion, drugs, and pre-marital sex. In the short span of this conversation, Betty was able to state that if she had been young during the 1970s she probably would have tried marijuana and that her children probably had. She called the Supreme Court decision in *Roe v. Wade* a "great, great, decision," something which she had done before. As Betty had discussed both topics before, there was no new controversy that could emerge from these particular issues. Then, Safer dropped the bomb by asking, "what if Susan Ford came to you and said, 'mother, I'm having an affair?'"[3] Betty, in typically honest fashion responded that she would not be surprised since Susan was a perfectly normal human being and was like all young girls. She added that if Susan did come to her, she would give her advice and support. She went on to say that she felt Susan was a little young to start having affairs. Betty had not intended to endorse premarital sex (she was still somewhat old fashioned in her beliefs). Her intent was to be open minded and to show compassion for her daughter in this hypothetical scenario — the result was to open a flood gate of controversy.

Initial response was overwhelmingly negative and hostile with comments such as "you are no lady — first — second — or last. Keep your stupid views to yourself from now on."[4] Another individual commented, "our recent history has seen this nation's First Ladies dedicating themselves to restoring the White House; beautifying America; and remaining silent. You, Mrs. Ford, should take an example from this latter group."[5] Gearing up for the 1976 election and vying for his party's nomination, her husband suggested that her comments had cost him 10 million votes — upon further reflection, and seeing the quotes in the paper, he amended the figure to 20 million lost votes. The politically astute Donald Rumsfeld happened to be witnessing the interaction between Betty and Jerry and had to interject. He felt the president was off target — he thought that her statements would result in a thirty million vote gain.

While initial response to the interview was overwhelmingly negative, in the long run, the frankness and refreshing honesty shown by Mrs. Ford during the interview actually boosted her popularity. One woman wrote:

> I am 83 years old, and one of my friends calls me the last of the Puritans. I haven't been able to decide what our society should do about abortion, and sex relations, and marijuana. But I do know what I think about honesty. I'm for it. And I am deeply grateful that we someone in the White House who thinks integrity is more important than political advantage. Many thanks for your refreshing example.[6]

More support poured in! Even those who did not agree with her views felt she was a positive role model for democracy and free thought. One St. Louis radio station aired the following commentary (despite the fact that they had continuously campaigned against ERA):

> We heartily approve of Mrs. Ford's working for passage of ERA or any other political goal ...When we start regarding political activity by a first lady, or any citizen, as "demeaning," our democracy is in big trouble.[7]

Rumsfeld was apparently right — what had initially seemed like a disaster for the reelection campaign had actually turned out to be something of a positive. As time went on, some campaign buttons even stated *Let's Keep Betty's Husband in*

104 Jeffrey S. Ashley

the White House. America liked their first lady and Betty was certainly an asset for the campaign.

Not everything centered around the campaign, however. Not long after the Morley Safer interview had aired, there was an attempt on President Ford's life. On September 5, 1975, Jerry was in California having just met with Governor Jerry Brown. It was after their meeting that Jerry took the opportunity to soak up some California sun and meet with a large number of apparent supporters. He was walking along through the crowd shaking hands with people when a woman dressed in red suddenly pulled out a gun and pointed it at the president. At first, Jerry thought she was shoving her hand forward for him to shake — until he saw the pistol — she was that close. The secret service detail was quick to act and was able to wrestle the woman, Lynette (Squeaky) Fromme, to the ground before she was able to fire a shot. Nobody was hurt, but word made it to Betty back at the White House. She learned that Jerry was okay and that the situation was resolved. She initially felt relieved and went about her business. After a few hours, however, it hit her — Jerry had been in danger. While in the back of her mind she knew that this was always going to be a possibility, it didn't really hit home until there was an actual threat. She loved her husband and did not want anything to happen to him — she was worried.

Only seventeen days later, she had cause for concern once again. This time there were shots fired. Once again, Jerry was in California. He was in San Francisco coming out of his hotel when suddenly there was a gunshot. Secret Service agents covered Jerry and ushered him into his car where they sped to the airport. His assailant, Sara Jane Moore, had ties to a number of radical organizations operating in northern California and had decided to take an extremely radical approach to public policy — murder. Fortunately, someone in the crowd saw her gun and was able to deflect her aim just in time. As with the Fromme incident, nobody was hurt. Jerry's response was to face the cameras that evening and tell reporters and all of America that he was okay and that he was going to continue operating as their president. He insisted that there was supposed to be a connection between the people and their leader and that shaking hands and meeting the masses was an integral part of that relationship. He was not going to cower down to "an infinitesimal number of people who want to destroy everything that's best about America."[8]

He was able to use the events and the media to his advantage — he looked danger in the eye and was not afraid. For at least one evening, the media was on his side.

Other media incidents did not turn out as well as Jerry's post assassination attempt briefing or Betty's *60 Minutes* interview (which was fine in time). Several

Election Hopes

reports that came out toward the end of the campaign made it harder and harder for Jerry to distance himself from the shadow of Nixon and the scandal of Watergate as election-day neared. These tended to distract voters and sway their attention away from his record of accomplishment during the time he was president. While his opponent, Jimmy Carter, was positioning himself as the champion of the moral good and the person we needed to restore ethics to government, Jerry Ford was finding it increasingly difficult to do the same. Despite the fact that Jerry *was* a good person who was committed to morality and propriety, his leadership and commitment were being questioned.

With the media circus that seemed to follow him and with the constant Watergate cloud that seemed to hover over him, it was a challenge for Jerry to simply get nominated by his own party. His years of service were not enough to simply give him the nomination. Even being the sitting president did not guarantee that he would become the Republican nominee and he was going to face a tough competitor in California Governor, Ronald Reagan (who would one day become President of the United States). Reagan was a charismatic figure who had once been a movie actor. He had poise and was able to captivate an audience in front of a camera. He was also from the West. As the campaign moved forward, it became apparent that the major difference between the candidates was regional rather than ideological. While they did differ over America's global role and Ford's policy of détente (Reagan was particularly critical of negotiations over a new Panama Canal Treaty), they both agreed that the national government should play a limited role in domestic affairs. With their positions being fairly similar, Reagan decided to go after Jerry's character and to try and keep the Ford name linked to Nixon and Watergate. Nixon cast doubt on Jerry's leadership capacity and questioned his abilities and accomplishments. By the time the Republican convention rolled around, Jerry and Reagan were hardly the best of friends. In fact, Jerry did not like Reagan at all. Despite the close campaign, Ford received the nomination by a close vote of 1,187 to 1,070 and set his sights on the Democratic candidate, Jimmy Carter. Unfortunately, the campaign would suffer several setbacks in the crucial months leading up to the November election.

One incident involved a member of the cabinet — Agriculture Secretary Earl Butz (an unfortunate holdover from the Nixon administration). While doing a story on the Republican convention, a *Rolling Stone* reporter, former White House staffer John Dean, wrote about a conversation that took place aboard an airplane headed for California. In this conversation, Dean revealed that a "shirt-sleeved cabinet member" had made a number of very disparaging remarks about African Americans. In Dean's story, the graphic language used by this "distinguished" cabinet member was laid out for all of America to see. It didn't take the

Washington press corp long to figure out that the unnamed person was Earl Butz since he was the only person that was known to use obscene language. The story was then carried by all of the major news sources and was responsible for triggering a firestorm among the black community. Many in the Washington establishment wanted Butz's head and he was clearly a liability for any election attempts. President Ford summoned Butz to the White House and immediately chastised and severely reprimanded him for language that was personally offensive and inexcusable from any member of his cabinet. Butz took his dressing down and offered to issue a public apology. This wasn't enough for many of Jerry's advisors who suggested that he fire Butz immediately. That was not Jerry's style — he felt a certain sense of loyalty to all of his people and he didn't want to react too quickly. Ultimately, Ford did ask for the resignation of Butz and it was Betty who convinced him. The comments made by Butz were racially offensive and carried sexist connotations that Betty would not tolerate. Butz was gone, but damage had been done.

Other media revelations were minor compared to the escalation of the Butz affair, but were also damaging while Jerry was trying to portray himself as being a remedy for the public perception that government was corrupt. There were reports that Jerry, while a member of Congress, had received a number of perks that might seem, to some, to be indications of corruption and impropriety. Jerry admitted to accepting free golf vacations and plane tickets from some of his friends in the private sector. While these were small tokens, and they were from friends, anything that might appear to be an indication of corrupt activity was being magnified during this election. Watergate was still fresh in the minds of America and the victor in this election would have to come across as "squeaky clean." That the investigation into Watergate seemed to drag on forever did not help Jerry in his election efforts. While he was eventually cleared of charges that he had misused campaign funds during his many congressional races, the investigation kept his name under a shadow of doubt for some time. Rumors that Ford had been recruited for the vice presidency because of his congressional ties never disappeared either. While there has never been any proof, there had been speculation that Jerry had been brought on board to put a stop to early Watergate investigations coming out of Congress. Former Nixon advisor, John Dean, kept these rumors alive during the latter part of the Ford election campaign because he thought that the revelation of further scandal might help the sales of a "tell all" book that he had just written entitled *Blind Ambition.*

Ford began the fall campaign as an underdog. Despite the fact that he was the sitting president, he had many things working against him. First, the primary had left the party divided. Reagan's attacks and unwillingness to concede left the party in disarray. Since this was the party associated with Nixon, they needed to be more unified than ever and they were not. In Jimmy Carter, the president was facing an opponent backed by a unified party that gave their man full support. Recent problems with Watergate and the use of campaign funds had resulted in new legislation that curbed party spending. Ford did not have the traditional Republican spending advantage when he went against Carter. The problems with the media and his inability to cleanly break from any semblance of impropriety also caused Jerry problems. Added to the mix was the fact that the economy was struggling and that Jerry did not seem to have very strong showings when he and Carter squared off against one another in debates. With everything that was working against him, simply being the president was not going to be enough. The final straw, however, was probably the pardon that he granted Richard Nixon. Jerry, Betty, and the rest of the family have always been convinced that this single act, more than any other, probably doomed any election attempt. While it may have been the right thing to do to move the country forward in its healing process, it did not sit well with the American public. Nonetheless, many Americans admired Ford's decency and honesty — just not enough. Ultimately, Ford lost the election by a relatively narrow margin and became the first president in 44 years to be removed from office through the election process.

The campaign had been hard fought and everyone in the family had pitched in. Betty had traveled across the country on Jerry's behalf (both alone and with him). And their son, Jack, had taken on a very active role in the campaign. They never let up and were campaigning right up until the very end. They were exhausted and Jerry had talked so much that his voice was gone. When it came time for the Ford campaign to graciously concede defeat, a member of the family had to read the speech for Jerry. Who else? Betty Ford! After thanking all of the people who had helped the family during the campaign, Betty faced the cameras and all of America in order to serve as Jerry's voice. She read,

Dear Jimmy, It is apparent that you have won our long and intense struggle for the Presidency. I congratulate you on your victory. As one who has been honored to serve the people of this great land both in Congress and as President, I believe that we must now put the division of the campaign behind us and unite the country once again in the common pursuit of peace and prosperity. I want to assure you that you will have my complete and wholehearted support as you take the oath of office this January. I also pledge to you that I and all members of my Administration will do all that we can to ensure that you begin your term as smoothly and as effectively as possible. May God bless you and your family as you undertake your new responsibilities.[9]

Reading the telegram through all of the emotions that the family were feeling was definitely a challenge. As always, Betty performed with grace and dignity. Jerry would later recall how proud he was of her for taking charge in such a tough moment. It really should not have been a surprise, however, since she had been doing it for most of her life. She would need to call upon all of her experiences and her inner strength once again as the Fords were about to leave Washington and politics for new challenges.

Election Hopes

PART 3: POST-WHITE HOUSE

Chapter 12

A NEW LIFE

When the Fords left the White House, Betty felt a certain amount of pending doom. While she had dreamed of a life away from politics, it was also the only life that she and Jerry knew together. Politics had been a part of their married life even before the actual marriage ceremony and Betty wasn't sure how she would handle life outside of Washington, D.C. On one hand, she was elated to finally have her husband to herself. On the other hand, after living as first lady for two and one-half years, she couldn't help but feel like her life was going down the drain. In some ways, she may have been right.

January of 1977 saw the Fords in unfamiliar territory out of politics. For Betty, it meant that she had her husband largely to herself for the first time in their marriage. It also meant that she had more time on her hands to fill. In Betty's case, this may not have been the best thing. The life that she had anticipated did not turn out exactly as she had planned. Instead of having her husband to herself, she found herself alone much of the time. The merry life of retirement in Palm Springs was pushing Betty deeper and deeper into depression. Jerry was away attending board meetings or golfing most of the time, all of the children were out of the house, and she missed her friends from Washington. Being fairly new to the area, they really hadn't had the time to develop any meaningful relationships as they had during their many years in the capitol. To deal with the sense of isolation, Betty began to drink fairly heavily and was mixing her alcohol with the prescription pain medication that she had been using for years.

That she was able to function at a high level for so many years only meant that she was adept at hiding her disease. She had been taking more and more medication beginning with the prescription she received for her pinched nerve in the late 1960's. Her "little pick me ups" were a mainstay throughout her time in the White House. As the pressure built during the assassination attempts, the numerous interviews, and a hectic campaign, Betty coped through increasing her dosage and self-medicating. She showed signs of a problem, but nobody seemed to pay much attention. When she would move slowly and would slur her words, aides and family members attributed the symptoms to fatigue rather than substance abuse. After all, she seemed to be functioning fine so she couldn't have a problem. Moreover, she was a strong person and, at the time, the general public sentiment was that only those who lacked willpower could fall victim to substance abuse.

Retirement and isolation really only accelerated a condition that had been present in Betty for years — she was an addict and an alcoholic. With no causes to pursue, no meetings to attend, and no social functions to plan, Betty filled the void with substance abuse. She began to isolate herself from others, pull down the blinds, and drown her sorrows. The once socially active Betty Ford was keeping to herself and turning down invitations to go places. She would claim to be ill or would come up with some other reason for not wanting to leave the house or to be seen in public. Above all, she did not want to interact with people because, while she wouldn't admit to having a problem, her ability to keep up appearances was rapidly diminishing. Even Jerry started to decline invitations for her — sometimes without her even knowing that one had been offered. He also noticed that her ability to function was diminishing, but he didn't really know what to do other than to further enable her by covering up the problem and assisting with the excuse making. In many ways, Jerry blamed himself for Betty's problems. He realized that his busy schedule over the years had placed a tremendous amount of pressure on Betty. Despite the fact that she had probably been born with the disease of alcoholism, the pressures of being married to Jerry Ford may have, in his mind, accelerated the problem. His solution was to shelter her from the outside. Such masking was becoming increasingly difficult.

Her occasional bouts with slurred speech and lethargic demeanor were easier to hide when she was in the White House — they could schedule around her. Out of Washington, however, she didn't have the large number of aides to help keep her problem out of the public eye. An ill-fated journey to Russia in the fall of 1977 is a case in point. Betty and Jerry had been hired by NBC to appear on a number of television shows covering a variety of topics. As a former dancer, Betty was asked to go to Russia to serve as a guest commentator and narrator for a production of the *Nutcracker*. While she was at home around dancers, sitting alone with a number of television cameras pointed at her was terribly unsettling. Her natural tendency to become nervous around the media was re-emerging and she attempted to calm herself through medication. Each time that she was excused from the taping, she would go to the restroom and take a pill. Over time, the cumulative effect of all the pills was showing and Betty was clearly not herself. When the show was broadcast in America, the press noticed immediately and reported that she was "sloe-eyed and sleepy-tongued."[1] This was just a euphemistic way of saying she was inebriated. While Betty was fortunate enough to have never seen the reviews — they were intentionally kept from her — she did see the show for herself. She realized that she had done a horrible job and was somewhat embarrassed. She would later ask Jerry if he had been embarrassed too and he diplomatically replied that she hadn't done her best, but he didn't want to mention that she was clearly sedated because he thought it might hurt her feelings. He also told her he didn't mention it because he, like the rest of the family, didn't want to face the facts. To acknowledge that she had done her job under the influence of drugs would force him to recognize that she had a problem — something he was not ready to do. By 1978, however, it was abundantly clear that Betty had a problem that the family could no longer ignore.

The first family member to take notice, and take action, was Susan. Susan had been working with Dr. Joe Cruse, a recovering alcoholic, at a treatment facility for children and asked if he would help her approach Betty. He said that he would be happy to help and, together, they confronted her mother and suggested that, perhaps, Betty had a problem with her pain medication. Betty, as many in denial about a disease do, refused to admit that there was any sort of a problem. In fact, Betty stated that she was in the process of cutting back on a couple of her pills. Betty was furious with her daughter. She called Susan a monster and told her that she simply didn't know what she was talking about and that she should leave. Susan was deeply hurt by the event but realized that things might be even worse than she had initially thought. Not to be deterred, Susan moved forward in her attempt to get her mother some help.

Despite Betty's response to the initial intervention, Joe Cruse was still very much a part of Susan's plans. Cruse, like Susan, realized that they would need to get more people involved if they were ever going to reach Betty and get her to truly listen to their concerns. Cruse decided to enlist the help of Dr. Joe Pursch from the Long Beach Naval Hospital nearby. The hospital had a substance abuse program and Dr. Pursch was experienced in prepping families for interventions. Pursch, in turn, brought in one of his nurses, Pat Benedict, who was a recovering alcoholic experienced in helping others to overcome their addictions.

After the initial intervention, Clara Powell was the only member of the small group that Betty appeared to respond to. The new intervention team believed, and rightly so, that they would need everyone close to Betty to stand together as a united front. Clara would have to be involved. Clara, who had been brought in under the guise of helping the Fords move into their new home, was still in town and was asked to stay in place for future intervention attempts — she agreed.

Pursch, Cruse, and Susan also realized that they would need to get every member of the Ford family involved. For most of the Ford clan, this meant changing their schedules to accommodate Susan's plan. Jerry, as the former president, was making a tremendous amount of money as a consultant and public speaker and was regularly booked. Bob Barrett and Jerry Ford got a call while they were in Rochester, NY in the midst of a speaking tour. Jerry was scheduled to Speak in Virginia and New York, but was able to enlist the help of Henry Kissinger. Kissinger agreed to step in and make the talks in Ford's place which allowed Jerry and Bob Barrett to fly home to California. With Jerry and Susan in place, it was just a matter of getting the other three immediate family members to come to Palm Springs.

Jerry called Mike and his wife Gayle and asked them to get to Palm Springs as quickly as they could. After Susan had urgently summoned Jerry home, he took his turn at recruiting the other members of the family. According to Mike, Jerry told him that in order for the intervention to work, there had to be a concerted effort and that the whole event "would be an act of love to help Mother and the family."[2] Mike and Gayle agreed and flew in to Palm Springs to help.

Steve Ford didn't really spend that much time around his parents in Palm Springs and wasn't aware that any real problem existed. He knew, as did all of the family, that something was amiss with Betty, but living away from the situation allowed him to turn his back on the problem and ignore it. He and his brother Jack had long since stopped coming down to spend the weekends because household tensions were running so high. Jerry was frustrated with how slow she moved and how long it took her to do even simple things like getting dressed. She was so slow-moving that even her next door neighbor had stopped inviting her over for lunch because it took so long for Betty to eat that other guests grew impatient. Steve didn't want to be around to witness his mother's decline and the strain that was beginning to show in his parents' relationship. Nevertheless, when asked to come down to participate in a family intervention, Steve agreed — even though he, like most of the family didn't really know what an intervention entailed.

The only family member to balk at the idea was Jack. It wasn't that he didn't love his mother or that he didn't think she might have some sort of a problem, but more that he felt that it might hurt her. He silently hoped that her problem would correct itself and questioned whether having everyone there at once might be extreme. To him, the intervention strategy was like rubbing salt into an open wound. His mother was clearly suffering, what good would having everybody gang up on her really do? Despite his initial reluctance, Jack was eventually

A New Life 117

convinced that an intervention was the only way to save his mother and he, like all of the others, ventured to Palm Springs for the confrontation.

At 7:30 on the morning of April 1, 1978, only two days after Susan and Dr. Cruse had first approached Betty about her condition, the entire Ford family (except Betty) was assembled in the former president's new office. They were being coached on the art of drug and alcohol intervention by Dr. Pursch, Dr. Cruse, and Pat Benedict. At first, the family began to take shots at one another and started to assess blame. Given their fear over the potential reactions to what they were about to do, Dr. Pursch knew that this was understandable. He also knew that the intervention had to happen if Betty Ford were to survive. He hadn't actually seen her as a patient, but by looking over her list of medications and listening to her symptoms, he knew that she was in bad shape. After the initial bickering between family members, it didn't take long for them to understand what they were about to do and how they were to proceed. Dr. Pursch scripted the entire intervention and had them all write down, in advance, what they were going to say. He wanted them to firmly, yet lovingly, tell Betty what she was doing to herself and what she was doing to each of them. In addition, he had each family member write down a list of specific events where Betty's drinking or drug use had caused them harm or embarrassment and how they felt about it. Pursch went on to explain that Betty would likely get mad, might walk out, and would certainly make excuses and lash out. He emphasized the importance of not letting her leave and not relenting in their pressure. They were all prepared for the fact that what they were about to say was going to hurt Betty tremendously. They were also made to understand that this was her only chance. On the prospect of the intervention, Jerry would later say, "I knew I would hate the things I had to say, but I was relieved too. I was convinced this was the only way the situation could be turned around. It was a dead-end street, the way we were going."[3]

Within an hour of their "training session," the entire Ford family, along with Clara Powell, Joe Cruse, Joe Pursch, Pat Bennedict, and Bob Barrett, was assembled in the living room of Betty's new house. Betty Ford was sitting on the sofa with all of her family around her. It didn't take her long to realize that something was amiss — the family was great, but why were all of the other people here? Jerry started things off by telling Betty that the family had some things to discuss with her. He told her that she needed to listen carefully to what they had to say because they loved her and they were concerned. After this introduction, there was a brief moment when some of the intervention group weren't sure who was supposed to start. This didn't take long, however, as Jerry took charge. He simply pointed a finger at his son Mike and told him to begin. Through it all, Jerry took control of the intervention and the three professionals didn't have to say a word — something they felt was truly unusual and somewhat miraculous (especially for a group that had no prior training and had only been briefed for a short time an hour before).

Mike began by telling his mother that he loved her, but that things had to change. He stated how he, as the oldest, probably understood, better than his siblings, the pressure she had always lived under as a politician's wife trying to raise four children. However, the use of alcohol and drugs to relieve the pressure was ruining everything she had worked so hard to protect — namely her relationship with her family. He told her that not only was she threatening to lose her family and friends, but she was on the verge of killing herself. He emphasized that her life was precious and that he didn't want her to die. His wife, Gayle followed by adding that she wanted to start a family and that Betty might miss out on the joys of being a grandmother. Gayle told her that she wanted her children to grow up knowing Betty as a healthy, loving woman — something that would not be possible under her current condition. She made it clear that Betty would either not be around to experience the joy, or she would be in such bad shape that the grandchildren would not want to be around her. In either case, the only way that Betty would be able to experience the joys of being a grandmother would be for her to sober up.

The others followed with stories of how her drug and alcohol use had impacted them. Steve recounted a time when he and a girlfriend had come down to Palm Springs to keep Betty company when Jerry was away. He was excited about preparing dinner and taking care of his mother — her response was to tell him she wasn't hungry and to pour herself another drink. He had done the shopping, cooking, and setting of the table only to have his actions quickly dismissed. He was hurt and he let his mother know it during the intervention. Jack told her that he used to be afraid to bring friends over to the house because he didn't know what shape she would be in. She was an embarrassment.

Susan actually broke down and cried — unable to get anything out. She had been strong enough to organize the intervention and had tried to intervene a few days earlier, but this time emotions were running high. She couldn't get anything out for a while and both she and her mother were sobbing. Eventually, Susan was able to tell Betty how watching her destroy herself was ripping Susan apart. She discussed how watching her mother sit around without any friends was painful and how she finally realized that the family had been covering up the problem for years. Susan even told her that it took the advice of an outsider (one of Betty's secret service detail) for her to see that her mother was destroying herself. His words opened her eyes and she told her mother that the once graceful dancer that she so greatly admired had been replaced by a clumsy old woman who needed help walking and who was injuring herself by her inability to remain upright while under the influence of drugs and alcohol.

Jerry mirrored these sentiments by recounting how Betty had fallen in the middle of the night and had cracked her ribs and chipped her tooth — because she was unable to control her drug and alcohol abuse. He even alluded to the fact that traveling frequently was made easier by the fact that he couldn't stand to watch her fall apart when he didn't know what to do about it. Jerry told her she had changed and was stuck in slow motion and unable to function normally.

Betty was shocked! All of these events and feelings came at her like a tidal wave and she was, understandably, overwhelmed. She was also angry. How ungrateful could these people be? She had sacrificed two careers and had always placed their needs ahead of hers. How could they possibly be saying such hurtful things and how could they be remembering such petty events? Betty was in denial and didn't want to see through to the fact that she *did* have a problem. Moreover, she didn't ever hear that they loved her — she only heard that she had failed them. For someone who had tried to follow in the footsteps of her strong mother, the prospect of failing her family was indescribably painful. Whether she agreed with them on the specifics, there was no denying that they had come together as a united front and that they were concerned. It was also apparent that they were not going to back down. Although she might not have been fully convinced that she was an addict and may have merely been trying to make the tension disappear, Betty agreed to enter into a treatment program at the Long Beach Naval Hospital.

This could have been kept a secret and Betty's addiction could have been brushed under the carpet. However, this was Betty Ford, the woman who had spoken her mind on controversial topics and had been very candid about her bout with breast cancer. Just as her decision to go public with cancer undoubtedly saved countless lives, her decision to tell the public that she was an addict and alcoholic took away some of the stigma attached to the disease. People suffering from chemical dependency at this time kept things hidden as much as possible — this was especially true for women. Betty Ford made it okay for many people to admit that they had problems and that they needed some help. After all, if Betty Ford, the very popular and highly regarded former first lady could have such a disease, so could anyone else.

The decision to tell the press came about as all Ford decisions did — through a family discussion. According to Steve Ford, "it was a team decision."[4] The "team" consisted of Betty Ford and the same people who had comprised the successful intervention team. Together, they decided that it would be a good move for Betty to announce that she was seeking treatment at the Long Beach Naval Hospital. Initially, however, Betty could only bring herself to admit to having a problem with her prescription pain medication. Apparently it was much harder for her to admit to any problems with alcohol. Ten days of therapy changed her mind. Betty began to realize that she was addicted to mood altering substances — not just pills — and that alcohol was as much of a problem for her as everything else. A second press conference was held while Betty was in treatment and several doctors announced that she was seeking help for alcohol addiction in addition to the pain pills for which she was initially admitted.

To this day, there are many people who insist that Betty wasn't a true alcoholic. This is because people do not understand the nature of alcoholism and they adhere to stereotypical images of gutter drunks and homeless bums. They fail to realize that there are millions of people who are functioning alcoholics that hold down jobs and even hold high levels of responsibility.

Habitual social drinkers can be alcoholics too — although clearly not all social drinkers are alcoholics. While Betty Ford never reached for a glass in the morning, never passed out in public, or never drank herself into oblivion for all to see, she was an alcoholic. Like many Americans she had long been a habitual social drinker who engaged in light drinking before dinner, had wine with dinner, and enjoyed having a nightcap. It never dawned on her that doing so might be habit forming. The habit became more dangerous when she mixed the light drinking with her pain pills. Doing so intensified the impact of each of them and could have led to serious reactions and, possibly, death. Fortunately, through the help of her family and the people at the Long Beach Naval Hospital, Betty was able to recognize for herself that she was an alcoholic — the opinions of others didn't matter. Betty was able to emerge from treatment as a sober woman for the first time in a great number of years and she was about to embark on a new, personally fulfilling stage of her life. Many of the wonderful things for which Betty Ford will eventually be remembered had yet to come.

Chapter 13

THE FORD LEGACY

When examining the Ford legacy in a book about Betty Ford, it is appropriate to look at both the accomplishments and lasting impact of Betty and her husband Jerry. He was the President of the United States and much of what he accomplished was made possible by the efforts of Betty. She allowed him to focus on his career while she took care of the household. Moreover, she was privy to many of the decisions that he was forced to make as the country's leader. While she wasn't able to influence him in every area, she certainly left her mark on many of them. They were, and are, a partnership — so much so that on a late 1990's Larry King interview, Jerry Ford was asked about his position on the Right to Choose. His reply was that *Betty and I* are Pro-Choice — he never even considered giving a reply as an individual. The Ford team approach was evident to many and, in 1999, *they* received the Congressional Gold Medal — an award that carries a tremendous amount of honor and prestige. To illustrate the intertwining of Jerry and Betty's lives, this award had been given to individual presidents in the past but had never been bestowed upon presidential partnerships. In this case, those in attendance were effusive in their praise for *both* President and Mrs. Ford with regard to their collective efforts to heal "a nation in torment."

JERRY'S LEGACY

Despite the fact that Jerry Ford was a member of Congress for many years and had a long career in the service of our country, he is generally remembered for only three things — and two of these are not necessarily flattering.

For better or worse, Gerald Ford will always be linked to the pardon of Richard Nixon shortly after he assumed the office of the president. There will always be those who suspect that Jerry was given the vice-presidency as some sort of a "deal." Public reactions to the pardon were mostly negative and the Ford family, and many political observers, feel that this single action may have contributed greatly to Ford's failed election attempt in 1976. Nevertheless, Ford has always remained firm in his conviction that it was the right thing to do. This was one decision that was made without unified family approval — but one he made without looking back. When asked by the U. S. House Committee on the Judiciary, Jerry swore that there were no secret deals connected with the pardon, but that it was his hope that such a move might end the nation's preoccupation with Watergate. He has always felt that the healing process of our government could not have happened if we were put through extended impeachment hearings. In many ways, this action can be viewed as extremely selfless on Ford's part since he sacrificed his own political career in order to move our country forward in the wake of Watergate.

Oddly enough, Jerry is also remembered as being a clutz and something of a bumbling oaf — both of which could not be further from the truth. Not only was he one of the most athletic people ever to ascend into the office of the president — he did turn down offers to play professional football — but he was one of the few who could walk into complex budget meetings without needing notes. He was a gifted athlete and he possessed a very sharp mind. Unfortunately a simple stumble down a flight of steps coming off of Airforce One and a simple misstep on the sidewalk were both captured on film and were broadcast over and over again. His perceived clumsiness was even the center of a Saturday Night Live parody done by comedian Chevy Chase who flailed about the stage posing as the president. His intelligence was even questioned at one point by an observer who commented that Gerald Ford played too much football without a helmet — again, a false notion. Nevertheless, despite the incredible inaccuracies of the images, they stuck with Ford throughout his time in office and afterward. In this case the legacy and the memories do not actually reflect the reality.

One area that does match reality to perception is in the area of honesty and integrity. The pardon of Nixon aside, Ford is remembered as a man of character. He was respected by members of both parties while a member of Congress and some feel it was his integrity, more than anything else, which made his appointment as vice president possible. In the wake of the Spiro Agnew fiasco, Nixon needed to have somebody who was beyond reproach. Confirmation was smoothed by the fact that he was trusted by just about everyone who knew him — if nothing else, Gerald Ford was an honest man. His honest, straightforward approach was refreshing in the post- Watergate atmosphere and is very much a part of his legacy. In an attempt to restore faith in the presidency, and all of government, Ford insisted that everyone around him remain as open as was possible. The result was that his administration was one of the most open in years — both Betty and Jerry had very candid relationships with the press and with the public. Betty's going public with her breast cancer is but one example. Unfortunately, no amount of honesty could have helped Jerry overcome the numerous obstacles he faced as he stepped into office.

His presidency was marked by quite a bit of inertia due, in large part, to the divided government created with his party affiliation running against a Democratic majority in both houses of the legislature. It was also hard for him to gain much momentum since the entire executive branch had been weakened by the Nixon administration's misconduct. Congress and the public were both out for blood and Jerry happened to be placed in the position that attracted most of their attention. Trying to deal effectively with a Congress that was increasingly assertive of its rights and powers was made worse by the fact that he inherited a number of problems for which there were no easy answers. Among the problems he encountered were a divisive war in Southeast Asia, a struggling economy, and the looming chance of widespread energy shortages.

Domestic policy under Ford is often remembered as being fairly lackluster. Not that Jerry didn't have a number of ideas to address the many problems our country was facing, he just had ideas that differed from the Democratic Congress. Ford's traditional conservative approach was to attempt modest tax and spending cuts and to push for deregulation of industry. Congress had other ideas. The result was that Ford was forced to rely on the veto in order to control spending and very few of his ideas were turned into policy without a great deal of compromise. These compromises did lead to bills dealing with energy control, tax cuts and the deregulation of the railroad and security industries (among other things), but ground-breaking change on the domestic front is not generally a part of Jerry's presidency. We will never know if things might have been different had he been elected in 1976.

Jerry fared a little better on the foreign front. While the United States and the Soviet Union were still very much involved in the Cold War, there were numerous arms talks between the two nations and the symbolic Apollo-Soyuz manned space flight took place under Ford's watch. Attempts and cooperation and agreement aside, Ford was able to retain a strong military presence. While Congress had passed the War Powers Act and there was a constant battle over presidential power in this area and in overseeing the CIA and covert operations, there was still an on-going suspicion about Russian military build-up. While Congress didn't want to lose control of military placement, they also weren't eager to diminish our capabilities. Cuts to any of the Ford Administration's military budget requests were minimal — one area where conflict didn't necessarily change the outcome.

Finally, Jerry served as head of state on numerous trips abroad — to China, Japan, and Europe — and helped to orchestrate the first international economic summit meeting. Given his orientation towards a more global perspective, the summit was clearly a victory and, while Ford isn't generally given proper credit, the meeting was a sign of things to come. Decades later, everything is done with economic globalization in mind. In short, Ford's administration did manage to accomplish some things that had a lasting impact — even though Jerry was facing numerous constraints entering into the office. Through it all, Betty was there!

BETTY'S LEGACY

Shortly after leaving the White House, Mrs. Ford once again found herself the unintended spokesperson for an illness that people never discussed openly. Instead of breast cancer, this time it was alcoholism and addiction. True to form, Mrs. Ford openly discussed her problem with reporters and the world, holding nothing back. Once again, her action had a tremendous spillover effect — if Betty Ford could have this problem, then it was okay for others to have it too. She brought the topic to the forefront and made it safe for people, especially women, to discuss the topic of addiction and to seek out help. As with her public discussion of cancer, her honest, open approach to handling personal adversity was turned into a positive. Her action helped to turn around and save the lives of countless individuals, and families of individuals, who had been suffering silently through addiction.

Betty had been given a second chance at life and she fully embraced it. While she was moving on with her new life, there were always reminders of what things used to be like. For example, close to a year after she had entered treatment, Jerry came home from a long trip and Betty offered him a drink to relax. She said, "A nightcap will relax you. Let me make you one." "No thanks," he said. "Come on," said Betty. "It will make you feel so much better, and I don't really mind." "I don't want one," he repeated. Betty didn't quite understand and remarked, "We always used to have a nightcap before we went to bed," she reminded him. "Yeah," he said. "And I never enjoyed it." She asked, "then why did you do it?" "Because," he said, "I didn't want you to drink alone."[1] A not-so-subtle reminder that she had once had a drinking problem and that it had impacted those around her. Jerry had covered for her by drinking when he didn't really enjoy it. He

The Ford Legacy   125

didn't have to anymore, and he didn't. Jerry stopped drinking that day too, and provided Betty with all of the support that she could possibly have hoped for. Betty was feeling better, her family was feeling better, and life was good. She wanted to pass this feeling along to others! Addiction and substance abuse became Betty's new cause (along with women's rights which she did not abandon).

She had her first opportunity to help another alcoholic about one year after she herself had discovered sobriety. Her next door neighbor and good friend, Leonard Firestone, was in trouble. The day was April 8, 1979, her birthday, and Nicky Firestone called to say that they would not be able to come over to the Fords for dinner. After telling Betty that Leonard was in terrible shape, Betty suggested that Nicky talk to Pat Benedict — the nurse who had played an instrumental role in Betty's recovery. As fortune would have it, Benedict was staying with the Fords for the weekend in order to celebrate Betty's birthday and first year of sobriety. Pat was happy to go over to the Firestone house to meet Leonard.

Firestone was the son of Harvey Firestone, the founder of Firestone Tire and Rubber Co. Being the son of a wealthy father allowed Firestone the opportunity to delve into areas that might not be accessible to other people. Some of these areas led to Jerry Ford and Leonard Firestone becoming good friends — by extension, their wives, Betty and Nicky also became close. Leonard was the chair person for the Nelson Rockefeller for President movement in 1964 and was a long-time moderate Republican cut from the same cloth as Jerry Ford. Their views were so closely aligned that Firestone's man, Rockefeller, was Jerry's vice president. Jerry's love of politics is clear, but Leonard Firestone enjoyed being active too — he even served as the U.S. Ambassador to Belgium. In short, Jerry and Leonard ran with the same crowd and had many mutual interests. One interest they apparently didn't share was alcohol abuse. Since the disease was a very sensitive issue in those days, any troubles that Mr. Firestone had were quietly covered up by his secretary and anyone else around him. He had attempted to quit on his own many times and had been having intermittent problems with alcohol for quite some time — he even went through treatment at Menninger's in Topeka, Kansas in 1965. After treatment, Firestone actually went nine years without a drink until he thought that he was "cured." Not understanding that alcoholics are never cured, he opened a vineyard in the Santa Ynez Valley. While the winery was a success, it probably wasn't the safest environment for a recovering alcoholic. He began to sample the wine and felt that a few sherries here and there wouldn't be too bad. The sherry led to martinis and, before he knew it, Firestone was out of control. He had been drinking rather heavily for a couple of years by the time Nicky made her desperate call to Betty Ford on April 8, 1979.

Pat Benedict, Betty Ford and some of the original cast that served at Betty's intervention worked their magic on a reluctant Leonard Firestone. Joe Pursch, Pat Benedict, Jerry Ford, and Nicky and Brooks Firestone (Leonard's son) convinced Leonard that he needed some help. Firestone offered to attend Alcoholics Anonymous, but the intervention team felt that he needed something more structured — at least initially. Jerry told him that he was his best friend and that he wasn't going to sit by and watch him die. Betty was a little more to the point — she *told* Leonard that he was going to go to treatment. He was ashamed, but Betty had helped to pave the way by going through the same thing a year earlier. In fact, she paved the way so much that he even told some of his friends and business associates that he was in rehab. When they asked what he meant, he said, "I'm doing the same thing Betty Ford did."[2] It was a good thing, because his "doing what Betty did" was crucial in setting up one of the most important and recognizable portions of Betty Ford's legacy.

After emerging from treatment, Leonard was caught up in the same spirit that had energized Betty — attempting to help other alcoholics who were in trouble. Together, they began to envision a treatment facility in Rancho Mirage, California. Betty and Leonard enlisted the help of Eisenhower Hospital Board President, John Sinn. He suggested to the hospital board that they all take a look at Betty's idea — they did, and told the three to give it a shot. For three years, they were busy raising funds and lobbying the California legislature to pass bills that would allow them to operate. With people such as Bob and Dolores Hope, Jerry and Betty Ford, and Nicky and Leonard Firestone, how could they fail? At one point, everyone who saw them coming knew that they were about to get asked for a contribution. They were very good at raising money — after one individual showed them how. A corporate executive informed them, after they asked him for $50,000, that they should always double what they really wanted. He gave them $100,000 and they took the lesson to heart — within three years, they had raised in excess of three million dollars. Jerry had worked his political magic to get the California legislature to pass the needed legislation (in only thirty days) and they were ready to roll. In October of 1981 they broke ground for the new facility and on October 3, 1982, The Betty Ford Center became a reality. The center is now one of the most famous and reputable treatment facilities in the world. While the center is mostly recognized for the number of celebrities who have sought treatment — among them are Kelsey Grammer, Elizabeth Taylor, Liza Minnelli, Johnny Cash, and Mary Tyler Moore — its real importance lies in the countless number of ordinary people who have benefitted from the center's existence. Everyone is treated as an equal at the center and everyone who wants it can gain from the programs that are offered. Many have wanted it, and many have been

The Ford Legacy

helped! The actions of Leonard Firestone and Betty Ford have created something that has been responsible for saving thousands of lives — a very significant legacy indeed.

While she is very proud of her accomplishments, she is also very humble. She continues to assert that she (and Jerry) are just ordinary people who emerged from ordinary backgrounds. Her sense of community and giving, however, can never be considered ordinary. She has always placed the well being of others before her own needs (sometimes to her own detriment) and has always done so willingly. She is a very socially conscious person who is troubled by what she sees as we enter into a new millennium. While she once referred to August 9, 1974 as her "saddest day," she has since amended that. She recently remarked that her saddest day is "today." Her concern is that media violence and the inability of today's youth to distinguish fantasy from reality is having an adverse impact on our future. Her concern is that children are not being allowed to grow up in a healthy environment and that something needs to be done. Her original saddest day stemmed from a realization that our country and system of government was in trouble. Her new saddest day stems from a concern that our entire society is in trouble and that our children need someone to step up, take charge, and protect them. Given her past, we might see Betty Ford at the forefront of a new cause!

From women's rights to the arts, and breast cancer awareness to drug and alcohol addiction, Betty Ford has never been afraid to openly discuss and champion a tough cause. In doing so she has opened doors which many might have never thought possible and she has been personally responsible for saving, or changing the lives of countless people both in this country and around the world. Through it all, she has never lost sight of her humble beginnings and she has never portrayed herself as being above anybody. It is this honest, humble, yet caring and daring approach which has endeared Betty Ford to generations of Americans. It is also this approach which has led to much of her success and has become very much a part of her personal legacy.

One can only wonder what lasting impact that both Betty and Jerry might have had if the election of 1976 had turned out differently. She would have been in the spotlight for at least another four years, and Jerry might have listened to some of her ideas for political appointments.

We will never know. What we do know is that, despite the fact that they lost the election, Betty Ford's straightforward, honest (though controversial) approach to politics and life had won the hearts of the public and had shaped the future of the office of the First Lady. Mrs. Ford had an impact and left behind a legacy — she made it possible and, in the eyes of some, even expected for the first lady to have an agenda and to speak out on political issues. In the words of reporter Mary Louis Oates, "Betty Ford was, and is, the bridge to the modern First Lady."[3]

Currently, Mrs. Ford can be found spending time with her husband, children, and grandchildren and she continues to oversee the operations of the Betty Ford Center in Rancho Mirage, California. She is also active in promoting women's rights, health care, and funding for substance abuse and has testified before Congress on numerous occasions. She has even spoken out against the policies of sitting administrations — even those of fellow Republicans. She was especially critical of President George Bush's "War on Drugs," which she viewed as extremely dangerous for a number of reasons. For one, she felt that the focus on cocaine and crack was making it so that problems related to alcohol were going largely unnoticed. Even more problematic, she told a House Aging subcommittee in 1991, was that the "war" was turning addiction into a crime. Such a regressive mind-set, she warned, would make it harder for people to come forward with problems and would make treatment facilities popular targets for funding cuts and program elimination. To this day, Betty Ford is still outspoken, candid, and extremely passionate about those causes she believes are worth fighting for.

Her activism and social impact has been profound. By continuously giving of herself, Mrs. Ford has been the recipient of over twenty prestigious awards including the Freedom of Human Spirit Award (International Center for the Disabled), the Hubert Humphrey Inspirational Award (The American Cancer Society), the Gold Key Award (National Council on Alcoholism), and the Presidential Medal of Freedom (awarded by President George Bush).

Finally, on October 17, 1999, she and Jerry received the Congressional Gold Medal that was mentioned previously. This is important to mention because this is something that Betty considers one of her proudest moments. After battling through the death of her father, divorce, the struggles of motherhood, mental distress, cancer and addiction — all in a very selfless manner — Betty was being recognized. Not as an individual (she wouldn't have liked that) but as a full and equal member of a partnership that weathered many storms and had battled through them to simply serve others to the best of their ability.

She would want to be remembered as simply "an ordinary woman who believed that my family came first."[4] However, the life she lived, the path that she paved for future first ladies, the lives she has touched, and the legacy she has created have ensured that she will long be remembered for much more. To anyone who has read about her, Betty Ford is a symbol of strength.

BIBLIOGRAPHY

Angel, Sherry, "This Ford has a Future," *50 Plus*, September 1986.

Anthony, Carl Sferrazza, "Still Candid and Caring," *Chicago Tribune*, July 11, 1993.

_____, "First Lady of Candor," *Washington Post*, April 8, 1993.

Arrington, Carl, "A Tough Love Cure For Chemical Dependency," *People Weekly*, October 1, 1984.

Ashley, Jeffrey S., "Betty Ford," In *American First Ladies*, (Pasadena, CA: Salem Press, 2002).

_____, "Betty Ford,"in *Laura Bush: Report to the First Lady* (Huntington, NY: Nova History Publications, 2001).

_____, "The Social and Political Influence of Betty Ford: Betty Bloomer Blossoms," *White House Studies*, September 2001.

Bergen, Candice, "An Intimate Look at the Fords," *Ladies Home Journal*, May 1975.

Betty Ford — Awards and Honors Received, http://www.lbjlib.utexas.edu/ford/grf/bbfaward.htm.

Beyette, Beverly, "Betty Ford, On Reflection," *Los Angeles Times*, January 18, 1989.

Boller, Paul F., Jr., *Presidential Wives*, (New York: Oxford University Press, 1988).

Bourne, Russell, "When the First Lady Speaks Her Mind," *American Heritage*, September 1987.

Bryant, Carleton R., "Betty Ford Rips War on Drugs," *Washington Times*, March 26, 1991.

Cassiday, Bruce, *Betty Ford: Woman of Courage*, (New York: Dale Books, 1978).

Chambers, Andrea, "Frank as Ever, Former First Lady Betty Ford Describes Her Harrowing Years of Addiction," *People Weekly*, March 9, 1987.

Colt, George Howe, "First Ladies; the Veterans of America's Second Toughest Job," *Life*, July 1986.

Feinman, Jeffrey, *Betty Ford*, (New York: Award Books, 1976).

Feldman, Trude B., "Gerald and Betty Ford: It's not the end of the World," *McCall's*, January 1977.

Ford, Betty with Chris Chase, *A Glad Awakening*, (New York: Doubleday, 1987).

Ford, Betty with Chris Chase, *The Times of My Life*, (New York: Harper and Row, 1978).

Ford, Gerald R., *A Time to Heal*, (New York: Harper and Row, 1979).

Frank, Elizabeth Pope, "Betty Ford's Secret Strength," *Good Housekeeping*, September 1978.

Gamarekian, Barbara, "Mrs. Ford Criticizes Neglect of Alcohol in U.S Drug Efforts," *New York Times*, March 26, 1991.

Gangelhoff, Bonnie, "Daughter Continues Betty Ford's Crusade Against Breast Cancer," *The Houston Post*, September 24, 1992.

Gould, Lewis L., ed., *American First Ladies*, (New York: Random House, 1995).

Kurylo, Elizabeth, "Cover Mental Illness, Ex-First Ladies Urge," *The Atlanta Constitution*, March 8, 1994.

Kinder, Gary, "Jack: The New Model Ford," *Good Housekeeping*, November 1975.

Liebman, Lisa, "New Woman People of the Year," *New Woman*, December, 1991.

Mac Pherson, Myra, "The Blooming Betty Ford," *McCall's*, September 1975.

McCarthy, Abigail, "First Helpmate: Influence in the White House," *Commonwealth* April 24, 1987.

Means, Marianne, "Mental Health vs. Health Care Reform," *Chicago Defender*, March 23, 1994.

Minton, Lynn, "Betty Ford Talks About Her Mother," *McCall's* May 1976.

Molino, Patricia, "Are You Alcohol Proof?: An Interview With Betty Ford," *Harper's Bazaar*, August 1985.

Nessen, Ron, *It Sure Looks Different From the Inside*, (Chicago: Playboy Press, 1978).

Oates, Marylousie, "The Political Wife — An Enduring Breed," *Los Angeles Times*, June 24, 1993.

Peer, Elizabeth, "Woman of the Year," *Newsweek*, December 29, 1975.

Robertson, Nan, "The Intimate Enemy: Will That Friendly Drink Betray You?" *Modern Maturity* February 1992.

Bibliography

Rohrer, Karen M., "'If There Was Anything You Forgot to Ask...': The Papers of Betty Ford," *Prologue: The Journal of the National Archives*, Summer 1987.

Schilling, Halle, "Health Coverage is Asked for Mental, Substance Ills," *The Boston Globe*, March 9, 1994.

Smith, Elizabeth Simpson, *Five First Ladies*, (New York: Walker and Co., 1986).

terHorst, Jerald F., *Gerald Ford: And the Future of the Presidency*, (New York: The Third Press, 1974).

Tobin, Leesa E., "Betty Ford as First Lady: A Woman for Women," *Presidential Studies Quarterly*, Fall 1990.

Warrick, Pamela, "Living Out Loud," *Los Angeles Times*, Nov. 12, 1995.

Watson, Robert P., *The Presidents' Wives*, (Boulder, CO: Lynne Reinner, 2000).

Weddington, Sarah, "Three Former First Ladies Speak Out," *Good Housekeeping*, February 1988.

Weidenfeld, Sheila Rabb, *First Lady's Lady*, (New York: G.P Putnam's Sons, 1979).

NOTES

CHAPTER ONE

[1] Ford, Betty, with Chris Chase, *The Times of My Life*, (New York: Harper and Row, 1978), p. 10.
[2] Ibid, p. 7.
[3] Ibid.
[4] Minton, Lynn, "Betty Ford Talks About Her Mother," *McCall's*, May 1976, p. 76.
[5] *Times of My Life*, p. 11
[6] Ibid. p. 7
[7] Betty Ford Talks About Her Mother, p. 76.
[8] *Times of My Life*, p. 17
[9] A&E Biography — Betty Ford

CHAPTER TWO

[1] *Times of My Life*, p. 16
[2] Ibid, p. 18
[3] Ibid, p. 21
[4] Ibid, p. 25
[5] Ibid, p. 24
[6] Ibid, p. 30
[7] A&E Biography
[8] Ibid.

CHAPTER THREE

[1] Ford, Gerald R., *A Time To Heal*, (New York: Harper and Row, 1979), p. 46.
[2] A&E Biography

134 Jeffrey S. Ashley

[3] *A Time To Heal*, p. 58
[4] A&E Biography
[5] *A Time To Heal*, p. 65

CHAPTER FOUR

[1] *Time to Heal*, p. 71.
[2] *Times of My Life*, p. 76.
[3] terHorst, Jerald F., *Gerald Ford: And the Future of the Presidency*, (New York: The Third Press, 1974), p. 68
[4] *Times of my Life*, p. 86
[5] Ibid, p. 90.

CHAPTER FIVE

[1] *Times of My Life*, 91.
[2] terHorst, pp. 72-73.
[3] *Times of My Life*, p. 93.
[4] Ibid. p. 95.
[5] Cassiday, Bruce *Betty Ford: Woman of Courage*, (New York: Dale Books, 1978), p. 42.
[6] Ford, Elizabeth, "Meet Capital's Not-So-VIPs," *Washington Post*, April 4, 1954, p. 95.

CHAPTER SIX

[1] *Times of My Life*, p. 118
[2] Ibid. p.119.
[3] *A Time to Heal*, p. 77
[4] *Times of My Life*, p. 124.
[5] Ibid., p. 125.
[6] Ibid., p. 143.
[7] *A Time to Heal*, p. 104.
[8] A&E Biography
[9] Tobin, Leesa E., "Betty Ford as First Lady: A Woman for Women," *Presidential Studies Quarterly*, Fall, 1990.
[10] Howard, Jane, "Forward Day by Day," *The New York Time Magazine*, December 8, 1974, p. 36.

CHAPTER SEVEN

[1] *A Time to Heal*, pp. 113-114.

Notes   135

[2] *Times of My Life*, p. 145.
[3] Ibid, p. 152.
[4] Ibid.
[5] *Times of My Life*, p. 151.
[6] *A Time to Heal*, p. 122.

CHAPTER EIGHT

[1] *Time to Heal*, p. 125.
[2] *Times of My Life*, p. 158.
[3] Personal Interview with Betty Ford, September 21, 2000. Transcript on file with author.

CHAPTER NINE

[1] *Times of My Life*, p. 230.
[2] *Betty Ford: Woman of Courage*, p. 117.

CHAPTER TEN

[1] *Times of My Life*, p. 186.
[2] "Betty Ford: Today Still Speaking Out," *Ms*, April 1984.
[3] Liebman, Lisa, "New Woman People of the Year," *New Woman*, December, 1991.
[4] *The Times of My Life*, p. 194.
[5] Kinder, Gary, "Jack: The New Model Ford," *Good Housekeeping*, November, 1975.
[6] *Times of My Life*, pp. 167-168.

CHAPTER ELEVEN

[1] *Times of My Life*, p. 1
[2] "Betty Ford: Today Still Speaking Out," *Ms*, April 1984.
[3] Excerpts from the interview transcript can be found in Sheila Rabb Weidenfeld, *First Lady's Lady: With the Fords at the White House*, (New York: G. P. Putnam's Sons, 1979), p. 173.
[4] Rohrer, Karen, "If There Was Anything You Forgot to Ask," *Prologue (Washington, DC*, Summer 1987.
[5] Ibid.
[6] Ibid.
[7] The quote is part of an editorial issued by a St. Louis radio station in response to charges by an Illinois representative's charges that Betty Ford's political activity on behalf of the ERA was "demeaning to the stature of the First Lady." As cited in Rohrer, "If There Was Anything You Forgot to Ask."

136 Jeffrey S. Ashley

[8] *A Time to Heal,* p. 312.
[9] Ibid, p. 435.

CHAPTER TWELVE

[1] Ford, Betty with Chris Chase, *A Glad Awakening,* (New York: Doubleday, 1987). P. 41
[2] Ibid, p. 14
[3] Ibid, p. 17
[4] Elizabeth Pope Frank, "Betty Ford: Her Secret Strength," *Good Housekeeping,* (September 1978), p. 91.

CHAPTER THIRTEEN

[1] *A Glad Awakening,* p. 124
[2] Ibid, p. 98.
[3] Oates, Mary Louis, "The Political Wife — An Enduring Breed," *Los Angeles Times,* June 24, 1993.
[4] Betty Ford Interview, September 21, 2000.

INDEX

#

25th Amendment, 63
60 minutes, 102

A

abortion, 71, 94, 102, 103
achievement, 62
activism, 94, 128
Adams, Abigail, viii
addiction, xi, 119, 120, 124, 125, 127, 128, 130
Admiralty House, 67
adolescence, 9, 15
adoption, 25
affect, 58
Agnew, Spiro Theodore, 61, 62, 122
agriculture, 105
alcohol abuse, 119, 125
alcoholic(s), 15, 114, 115, 119, 120, 125, 126
alcoholism, 15, 114, 120, 124
anger, 25
Anna Sokolow group, 16
Anthony, Susan B., 94
aptitude, 79
arms build-up, 76
arthritis, 58, 59, 84, 98
Arthur, Chester A., vii
arts, 7, 52, 94, 97, 98, 127
Asia, 123

assassination, viii, 104, 114
Astaire, Fred, 89
athletics, 26, 27
attention, 3, 8, 9, 13, 30, 60, 68, 70, 80, 97, 98, 105, 114, 123
Austria, 44
autobiography, 3, 14, 15, 20
average, 3, 26
awards, 128
awareness, xi, 96, 127

B

Belgium, 125
Bennington School of Dance, 16
Bennington, 16, 17, 18
Bernstein, Carl, 78
Betty Bloomer School of Dance, 12
Betty Ford Center, 126, 128
biography, xii, 40
black community, 106
Bloomer, Bill, 22
Bloomer, Elizabeth, 20
Boston, 22, 87, 131
Boy's Life, 41
boys, 7, 8, 13, 14, 40, 41, 43, 44, 45, 46, 49, 51, 52
Brazil, xiii
breast cancer, xi, 96, 102, 119, 123, 124, 127
brothers, 3, 5, 7, 8, 28
Brown, Jerry, 104

138   Index

Brussels, 83
Buchanan, James, vii
budgetary resources, viii
Bush, Barbara, viii
Bush, President George, 128
Butz, Earl, 105

C

cabinet members, 36, 76
California, 104, 105, 116, 126, 128
campaigning, 32, 107
cancer, xi, 28, 96, 98, 102, 119, 123, 124, 127, 128
carbon monoxide, 15
Carnegie Hall, 19
Carter, President Jimmy, 105, 107
Cavett, Dick, 70, 71
celebrities, 126
charity work, 17
Chase, Chris, 5, 21, 130, 141
childhood, 4, 6, 7, 8, 9, 15, 18, 31, 32, 41
children, 3, 4, 5, 6, 7, 11, 15, 16, 20, 26, 36,
    38, 40, 41, 42, 43, 44, 45, 46, 49, 50, 51,
    52, 53, 57, 58, 59, 60, 61, 63, 67, 68, 69,
    72, 79, 94, 97, 98, 99, 100, 102, 113,
    115, 118, 127, 128
Chin, Dr., 45, 46
China, 84, 124
choice, 54, 96
civic activities, 28
civic affairs, 50
Clinton, President William, vii
cocaine, 128
Cold War, 123
college, 13, 26, 27, 49
competition, 8, 14
conditioning, 39
conflict, 76, 124
confrontation, 21, 117
congress, iv, vii, xi, 35, 36, 37, 40, 42, 50, 61,
    62, 72, 75, 79, 91, 94, 95, 106, 107, 121,
    122, 123, 128
Congressional Club, 36, 37
congressional wives, 36, 37, 50

conscience, 23
conscious, 79, 127
conservatives, 31
constitution, viii, 63, 130
control, 4, 25, 99, 117, 119, 123, 124, 125
cooperation, 123
coping, 61
corruption, 106
Cowboy Artists, 87
crossing over, 44
Crown Drive, 42
Crown View, 42, 43, 49, 67, 70, 80, 86, 95
Cruse, Dr. Joe, 115
cub scouts, 52

D

dance, 7, 8, 9, 12, 13, 14, 16, 17, 18, 19, 20,
    22, 29, 31,44, 84, 87, 89, 90, 97
Darvon, 58
dating, 21, 28, 30, 31
Dean, John, 105, 106
Delaware, 57, 58
democracy, 103
denial, 115, 119
dependency, 119
depression, 8, 50, 69, 113
deregulation, 123
détente, 105
development, viii, xii, 42, 58, 79
Dewey, Thomas, 32
diamonds, 81
diet, 69
dinner parties, 90
disabled children, 98
divorce, 23, 29, 128
dreaming, 62
drinking, 15, 16, 21, 22, 29, 117, 120, 124,
    125
drive, 28, 30, 51, 58, 85
drug addiction, xi
drug use, 117
drugs, 61, 102, 115, 118, 119

Index

139

E

Eastern Europe, 83
education, 27, 36
Egypt, 87
Eisenhower, Mamie, 41
elections, 61
encouragement, 28
energy shortages, 123
engagement, 8, 20, 21, 31, 32
England, 87, 88
Episcopal Church, 11, 52
Equal Rights Amendment (ERA), 91, 94, 95, 97, 101, 102, 103
equal rights, vi, 91, 93, 94, 95, 97
Europe, 44, 45, 83, 124
exclusion, 13
excuse, 83, 114, 117
executive branch, 69, 77, 123
exercise, viii, 17, 42

F

Fairfax Park, 40
family, 3, 4, 5, 7, 8, 9, 11, 12, 15, 20, 23, 25, 27, 31, 35, 38, 39, 40, 41, 42, 43, 45, 46, 49, 50, 51, 52, 53, 54, 57, 58, 59, 60, 61, 62, 63, 67, 68, 70, 71, 72, 75, 77, 79, 80, 96, 97, 98, 99, 100, 102, 107, 108, 114, 115, 116, 117, 118, 119, 120, 122, 125, 128
father, 3, 4, 9, 11, 14, 15, 22, 25, 39, 44, 52, 59, 98, 99, 125, 128
Filipinos, 84
Finland, 83, 87, 89
Firestone, Leonard, 125, 126
First Lady, ii, xi, 74, 93, 97, 102, 127, 129, 130, 131
Fisher, Lillian, 6, 27
Florida, 35
Folsom, Frances Clara, ii
football, 7, 15, 17, 26, 27, 32, 51, 122
Ford administration, 77, 80, 86, 96
Ford library, 63

Ford, Jr., Gerald R., xi, 23, 25, 26, 27, 32, 36, 37, 40, 50, 53, 54, 62, 73, 75, 76, 95, 101, 122, 131
Ford, Michael Gerald, 39
Ford, Steven Meigs, 43
Founding Fathers, viii
Fountain Street Baptist Church, 20
France, 24
Franco, General, 83
Fromme, Lynette (Squeaky), 104
frustration, 17

G

Gamma Delta Tau, 13, 14
Gardner, John, 40
genetics, 39
Georgetown, 36, 40
Germany, 87
Godwin, Arthur Meigs, 43, 44
Godwin, Arthur, 21
Good Cheers, 14, 15, 23
Graham Crackers, 17
Graham, Martha, 17, 18, 19, 98
Grand Rapids, 3, 6, 8, 9, 13, 15, 17, 18, 19, 20, 22, 23, 25, 27, 28, 31, 32, 35, 37, 40, 44, 49, 50
Great Depression, 8, 11
Greece, 76

H

Halleck, Charlie, 58
Harris, Natalie, 16, 18
health care, 128
Hearst, Patty, 68
heart disease, 59
heavy, 18, 59, 89
helplessness, 45
Herpolsheimer's Department store, 12, 23, 20, 30, 50
high school, 16, 26, 36
Hoeven, Charles, 54, 58
Hollywood, 90

140 Index

honesty, xi, 26, 80, 102, 103, 107, 122
hostess, 24, 36, 84, 86, 91
House Judiciary Committee, 73, 95
House Minority Leader, 54, 59, 62
House of Representatives, 28, 54, 59, 69
Houston, 130
Howe, Nancy, 69, 85, 96
Hungarian uprising of 1956, 44

I

Idaho, 30
Illinois, xiii, 3
impeachment, 73, 122
inauguration, vii
individuality, xi, 79, 100
Indonesia, 84
inertia, 123
infinitesimal, 104
inflation, 76
infrastructure, 49
insight, xiii, 79
insulin, 22
integrity, 26, 80, 103, 122
intervention, 115, 116, 117, 118, 119, 126
intuition, 6
Iowa, 54
Iran, 87
Ireland, 87, 89
isolationism, 28
Israel, 76
Italy, 44

J

Jackson, Andrew, vii
Japan, 87, 124
Jefferson, Thomas, vii
Johnson, Lady Bird, 37
Jordan, 84, 85, 86

K

Kansas, 125

Kennedy, Jacqueline, viii, 24, 77
King Hussein, 84, 85
King, Jr., Martin Luther, 72
Kissinger, Henry, 116
knowledge, 62

L

Larry King interview, 121
law, 27, 28, 30, 39, 41, 42, 49, 61, 94
lead, 11, 20, 27, 54, 68, 123
leadership, 54, 105
learning curve, 36
learning, 36, 38
legislation, 94, 107, 126
lifestyle, 18, 19, 49
Long Beach Naval Hospital, 115, 119, 120
loyalty, 24, 89, 106

M

Madison, Dolly, 84
Madrid, 83
Manila, 84
manners, 6
Mantle, Mickey, 46
Marcos, Ferdinand, 84
Marcos, Imelda, 84
marijuana, 102, 103
marriage, 22, 23, 36, 39, 53, 113
married, vii, viii
Maryland, 62
mastectomy, 96
mean, 27, 52
media, 62, 70, 80, 81, 100, 101, 104, 105,
    106, 107, 114, 127
medication, 58, 113, 114, 115
Meet the Press, 72
Michigan, 3, 15, 20, 27, 28, 31, 32, 35, 37, 39,
    40, 42, 78, 95
military budget, 124
military build-up, 123
military presence, 123
Minority Leader, 59, 69

Index   141

model, 12, 17, 18, 31, 36, 37, 79, 80, 103
modeling, 18, 23
momentum, 123
money, 12, 15, 27, 44, 49, 59, 67, 95, 116, 126
Moore, Sara Jane, 104
morality, 105
mother, 3, 4, 5, 6, 7, 8, 9, 11, 12, 16, 17, 18, 19, 21, 25, 28, 29, 35, 50, 51, 52, 53, 54, 58, 59, 60, 61, 63, 71, 79, 89, 98, 102, 115, 116, 118, 119
muscles, 16
mutual, 125

N

name recognition, 27
National Endowment for the Arts, 69, 97
National Honor Society, 26
National Organization for Women (NOW), 94
national politics, 54
National Security Council, 88
National Security, 88
National Women's Party, 94
natural, 7, 19, 77, 94, 114
Navy, 28
Nebraska, 25
negative consequences, 47
nerve, 57, 58, 59, 84, 113
nervous breakdown, 60
nervousness, 101
New York, iii, 14, 16, 18, 19, 23, 31, 98, 116, 129, 130, 131, 141
Nixon, Pat, 85, 101
Nixon, President Richard, 61, 72, 73, 74, 76, 99, 107, 122
North Carolina, 28
November election, 105

O

offspring, 25
Ohio, 22
Olympic Games, 76

organization, 13

P

Palestinian Liberation Organization, 76
Palm Springs, 113, 116, 117, 118
Panama Canal Treaty, 105
Panama, 105
Parent Teacher Association (PTA), 50, 60
Paris Peace accords, 76
party leadership, 54
peacestone, 77
Pennsylvania Avenue, 80
perception, 106, 122
performance, 18
personal relations, 80
personality, 53
Philippines, 84
Poland, 83
political environment, 32, 61, 78
politicians, 38, 72
politics, 26, 27, 31, 32, 35, 36, 37, 38, 42, 53, 62, 75, 78, 86, 90, 108, 113, 125, 127
population, 84
Powell, Clara, 39, 60, 115, 117
pregnancy, 39, 40, 45, 46
pre-marital sex, 102
prescription pain medication, 113, 120
Presidential Medal of Freedom, 98, 128
presidential wives, vii, viii
primary election, 31
private sector, 106
production, 22, 114
professional training, 16
program, 50, 97, 115, 119, 128
protective, 15, 16
protocol, 38, 89
psychiatrist, 60, 61
public life, 49, 62
public policy, 104
public service, 42, 43
public speaking, 37
public support, 77
punishment, 53, 100

Q

Queen of England, 87, 88

R

radical, 54, 104
Reagan, Ronald, 105
recognition, vii, 27, 62
Red Cross, 28, 36, 69
refugees, 44
rehearsal, 31
relationships, 5, 29, 80, 113, 123
remorse, 4
Republican National Convention, 57
Republican Party, 54, 58, 60, 61, 62, 71
reputations, 84
response, 17, 71, 96, 100, 103, 104, 115, 118
Rockefeller, Nelson, 125
Roe v. Wade, 71, 102
Romania, 83
Rome, 83
Roosevelt, Franklin Delano (F.D.R.), 77
Royal Rubber company, 3
Rumsfeld, Donald, 59, 103
Russia, 114

S

Sadat, Anwar, 87
Safer, Morley, 102, 104
Salzburg, 83
sample, 125
Saturday Night Live, 122
Schafly, Phyllis, 95
Schlesinger, Arthur, 78
school, 4, 6, 13, 14, 16, 17, 18, 27, 28, 30, 39, 41, 50, 51, 52, 59, 68, 84, 93
secret service, 67, 68, 69, 70, 78, 95, 99, 104, 118
Security Council, 88
self, 7, 35, 54
self-medicating, 114
Senate, 62, 69, 72, 94

series, 9, 13, 73, 93
Shah of Iran, 87
shaping, 97
siblings, 7, 26, 118
sisters, 14
sobriety, 125
social functions, 37, 53, 114
social life, 15, 18, 20, 28, 68
socializing, 17, 41
South Pacific, 28
Southeast Asia, 123
Soviet Union, 76, 123
Spain, 44, 83
Speaker of the House, 38, 42, 54, 59
spending cuts, 123
spousal support, 60
stability, 22, 79
stages, xii
stars, 89
state dinners, 85, 86, 87, 89, 90
stepfather, 21, 28, 29, 35, 43
stock market, 8, 15
STOP ERA, 95
stress, 53, 61, 68, 73
substance abuse, 114, 115, 125, 128
suicide, 15
Sunday school teacher, 52
Supreme Court, 36, 71, 90, 94, 102
Symbionese Liberation Army (SLA), 68
symbol, xii, 40, 77, 86, 88, 91, 128
symptoms, 114, 117

T

tax evasion, 62
Tennessee, ii
theory, 29
thinking, 28, 49
Times of My Life, 3, 5, 14, 15, 40, 130, 141
traits, 9, 26
transformation, 97
traveling, 9, 15, 59, 72, 83, 101, 119
Travis, Calla, 8, 12, 13, 20
treatment, 21, 78, 115, 119, 120, 124, 125, 126, 128

Index

Truman, Harry, 76
trusted confidante, viii
Turkey, 76
Turks, 58, 59, 62
Tyler, John, vii

U

unemployment, 76
United Nations, vii
United States, iv, xi, 44, 61, 63, 73, 75, 76, 84, 94, 96, 99, 101, 105, 121, 123
universal, 5
University of Michigan, 27

V

Van Buren, Martin, vii
Vermont, 16, 17
Vice President, 62, 63, 67, 68, 69, 73
Vietnam, 76, 77
violence, 127
Virginia, 40, 42, 46, 70, 84, 116

W

Walters, Barbara, 70, 71, 93, 96
War Powers Act, 123
Warren, Bill, 9, 20, 21, 22, 23, 32
Washington Hospital for Sick Children, 98
Washington Post, 78, 81, 129
Washington, D.C., xi, 35, 113
Washington, Martha, viii
Watergate scandal, xi, 61
Watergate, xi, 61, 72, 73, 75, 78, 81, 96, 99, 105, 106, 107, 122, 123
Wellesley College, viii
West Germany, 83
White House, v, vi, vii, viii, ix, xi, 1, 15, 24, 38, 69, 72, 76, 78, 79, 83, 84, 85, 86, 87, 88, 89, 90, 93, 97, 98, 99, 101, 103, 104, 105, 111, 113, 114, 124, 129, 130
Whitefish Lake, 4, 5, 7, 8, 11
Wilkie, Wendell, 27
Wilmarth, Bud, 8, 14
Wilson, Woodrow, vii
women, viii, ix, xi, 18, 30, 58, 85, 86, 91, 93, 94, 95, 96, 97, 101, 102, 119, 124, 125, 127, 128
women's rights, xi, 95, 101, 125, 127, 128
Woodward, Bob, 78
workers, 69

Y

Yale School of Law, 27
Young Turks, 54
Young Yugoslavia, 83